LIVINGtouch

Marsha Spradlin

New Hope
Birmingham, Alabama

The stories told are true accounts of the author's experiences. The names have been changed to protect identities.

New Hope
Birmingham, Alabama

© 1988 New Hope
All Rights Reserved. Published 1989.
Printed in the United States of America.

Dewey Decimal Classification: 248.5

Subject Headings: WITNESSING

Library of Congress Cataloging-in-Publication Data

Spradlin, Marsha G., 1954-
    LIVINGtouch / Marsha Spradlin.
        p.   cm.
    Bibliography: p.
    ISBN 0-936625-72-4
    1. Women—Religious life. 2. Witness bearing (Christianity)
I. Title. II. Title: Living touch.
BV4527.S66 1989
248.8'43—dc20   89-9327
                                      CIP

N894105 • 12M • 0789

ISBN:0-936625-72-4

LIVINGtouch is dedicated to

Bobbie Sorrill—Thank you for encouraging me to write. Your desire to win others to our Father has blessed my life.
Michele Thomas, MD—Thank you for encouraging me to never give up hope. Together, with the Father's touch, we won!

Contents

Foreword

Why another book on evangelism, you might ask? Are not the shelves of bookstores filled with books on how to witness? Do Christians not just share their faith naturally and automatically? Obviously the answer to these last two questions is a resounding no!

LIVINGtouch is not just another book on evangelism. Nor is it a manual on how to witness. Rather, it is a "want to" book, a book filled with insights and inspiration that will make you want to witness.

Perhaps you are on the same personal, spiritual journey I am on. I have been a Christian for many years. Philosophically, theologically, and spiritually I believe the world is lost, that there are billions of persons all over the world who do not know Jesus Christ as Saviour and Lord. I know too, and believe with all my heart, that every Christian is commissioned by our Lord to be a witness for Him, to tell others Who He is and what He has done for us.

But in recent years I have gotten away from that commission and have begun to fill my life with doing "good things" for the Lord. Witnessing seemed to gravitate slowly but surely to the back burner of my life. In recent months the Father has changed my perspective. I sense a moving of the Holy Spirit in my own life and a growing conviction about the lostness of the world and my role in *sharing the good news* of *Jesus Christ*. With God's help, I am becoming a life-style witness, one who is touching lives again.

For me, therefore, *LIVINGtouch* is a book whose time has come. It came into my life when I needed the revival fires rekindled. I want with all my heart to touch lives for Jesus Christ and to be a witness for Him. This book will help you, as it has me, to explore your inner and outer worlds and to commit or recommit all that you are and do to helping others come to know Jesus Christ as Saviour and Lord. When you finish reading the book and close its cover, you will no doubt say as I did: "Wow! I want to witness, I can witness, and I will witness."

I am glad that Marsha Spradlin is my friend and co-worker. I know of no person who better models for me what it means to touch lives and to be a life-style witness. Therefore, Marsha has the credentials to write this book. This vibrant and gifted young woman has been a teacher, speaker, writer, and Christian consultant. She is presently on the staff of the Southern Baptist Woman's Missionary Union.

Dare to risk reading *LIVINGtouch*. The book will change your life and make you want to be a life-style witness. I commend this book to you.

BOBBIE SORRILL
Associate Executive Director, Missions Education System,
Woman's Missionary Union

I can't wait for you to read this book! Hurry, get a cup of coffee, sit down, and get ready for a life-changing experience. Your life will be touched . . . then . . . oh, I hope then, your life will become a LIVINGtouch. I laid the book down after reading it and thought, "I can do that. I must do that." As you get caught up on the stories of Marsha's journey with people in her life you will subtly realize that everywhere she goes, she shares Christ. You can't wait for the ending. You just know she will introduce each one, almost each one, to Christ.

As I read, my heart cheered her on, as if to encourage her as she gave her witness. Then the truth sank deep. It is easier to be a *spectator* Christian (a sideline Christian) than a *participator* Christian. Ouch! The author has just described most of us.

Go ahead! Read it anyway. You are going to love the chapter that deals with your circle of influence. This concept alone could change forever your understanding the imperative to witness, the responsibility to witness, and *your circle of influence*. You will be challenged to examine

• making choices that count,
• balancing inner life and external activity,
• risk-taking adventures,
• self-esteem rooted in God-esteem (my favorite).

The author of *LIVINGtouch* models for you all the truths presented in this inspirational and motivational book. When you put this book down, I hope you are saying, "I can do that. I must do that."

ESTHER BURROUGHS
National Consultant for Women, Home Mission Board

Preface
What Is a LIVINGtouch?

Jan was not intentionally eavesdropping, but it was obvious she had overheard every word of my conversation with Vicky, a waitress in a Dallas coffeeshop. Perhaps Jan had sensed openness and acceptance from the conversation. Perhaps she was lonely . . . so lonely that just visual contact with persons made her feel warmhearted.

I noticed Jan and felt she wanted an invitation to join Vicky and me at our table. As Vicky left to continue her responsibilities, I signaled Jan to join me. Moving quietly she said, "I heard what you told that waitress. Will it work for me too?"

I marveled at the presence of the Holy Spirit. I knew it was He who synchronized our lives to meet in this time and place. My new acquaintance with Jan reinforced my conviction that people are starved for answers regarding life. Only God has answers to life's perplexities.

What Jan overheard was only one of a series of 15-minute visits with Vicky. For over a year I had frequently stopped for coffee before going to work. It was through such visits that Vicky and I became acquainted. Although our visits covered a variety of topics, our conversation this morning was about God. I had just shared with Vicky God's plan of salvation. It was now evident to me that this morning's witness to Vicky was a vicarious witness to Jan.

As Jan introduced herself, I noticed a real quiver in her voice. She seemed shy and afraid. She had an inner beauty and I noticed real potential. It was not long until I knew some of Jan's background, life-style, and struggles. Her emotions were tender. She appeared to be desperate for love and attention.

"On this very morning," she said, "I tried to kill myself." Jan shared why she had lost hope. She did have some real problems.

It sounds trite, but I am convinced God is bigger than any problem we have. As I shared this with Jan, I realized there was a spark of hope. After an hour with her, I recognized that Jan faced many decisions, but the most important decision was concerning her personal relationship with Jesus Christ. I walked Jan to her car. I slipped a New Testament into her small hand. I focused my eyes intensely on hers and said, "I love you."

She sat in her parked car with her head buried in her hands for what seemed to be a long time. I observed her from my car and prayed she was putting her trust in Jesus Christ. As she drove away, I immediately realized I might never see her again. I also realized that through Jesus Christ we could spend eternity together for we had just encountered His LIVINGtouch.[1]

My encounter with Jan in 1984 made me more convinced than ever that the reason for our very existence is to have a LIVINGtouch encounter with ordinary people on ordinary days. I am equally convinced the reason you bought this book is because you, too, share a desperate heart to fulfill the Great Commission and become a LIVINGtouch witness in your world. Perhaps you are concerned about a friend, a family member, or a significant other in your life who is lost.

Maybe you are aware that as you read these pages multitudes of people are dying without Christ. It is obvious that you join me and thousands of others who are being encouraged. Studies report that more Christians—maybe as many as 98 percent—are beginning to share their faith with others.[2]

In order to make a real difference in our world we, that's each of us, must make sharing Christ a priority—an exciting way of life. We must recognize that making an impact in the world for Christ means taking a bold approach that involves risk—change. No longer can we afford ourselves the luxury to sit contentedly in our church pews pondering why more isn't being done to win the lost world. Instead, we must look at ourselves. Such introspection can lead to a discovery of your distinctive gifts and abilities that makes you different from your brothers and sisters in Christ—even the ones sitting next to you in church.

When we recognize and celebrate our individual gifts and abilities we become available to touch the lives of others. I believe the church can make a LIVINGtouch difference in the world. As we utilize our unique gifts and abilities, touching the world for Christ becomes personal and possible, but it will take all of us.

I wish I could say this book would give five or ten simple steps for winning the world for Christ. I wish I could say that these steps would transform the world. Yet, in all my research, observation, and study of the Scriptures, I see no specific steps regarding being a personal witness. What I have discovered is that witnessing starts with touching lives. Perhaps that discovery is what makes this book different than most books on the personal witnessing topic. It is not a "how-to" book; it is a "being" book. As I learn to be like the Father, I automatically touch lives and win others to Him. As I emulate Him I become a LIVINGtouch.

As I researched the Scriptures to find out how Jesus made a difference in His world, I found no set of steps. Instead I discovered His LIVINGtouch.

- "If only I touch his cloak, I will get well" (Matt. 9:21).
- "It is I myself. Feel me, and you will know" (Luke 24:39).
- "And all who touched it were made well" (Matt. 14:36).
- "Jesus asked, 'Who touched me?' " (Luke 8:45).

If we choose to make a difference in the world, we must learn to touch as Jesus touched. His touch was daily and in the ordinary moments of life. His touch was consistent. His touch came from deep within.

If we choose to make a difference in the world, we must join together, as individual believers that are not afraid to touch. It is to you that this book is dedicated.

Perhaps no book, or even thought, is original. Even though Thomas Edison held more than 1,000 patents, he claimed only one original invention—the phonograph. All other inventions were simply adaptations upon ideas of others. Many original ideas, even on personal witnessing, may really be exploring and improving upon ideas of others.

LIVINGtouch is an attempt to explore personal witness beyond the boundaries of "hit-and-run" experiences, giving out tracts, and learning five to ten steps that will ensure results. It is my conviction that as we become related rightly internally, we can become related rightly externally. We begin to touch the lives of our neighbor and our neighbor's neighbor through our everyday encounters.

In the chapters to follow you will have the opportunity to examine carefully who you are. The book is divided into two parts. Part 1 explores the internal world as we deal with the dimensions and characteristics of those seeking to make a winning witness. Part 2 focuses on the external world or the external self. Practical helps and guidance will be explored in each part.

Each chapter will include a LIVINGtouch encounter, a real story that parallels with the content that follows. Feel free to agree and even disagree. The important thing is to think. "The Challenge to Touch" is the application portion of each chapter. This section highlights important thoughts and concepts explored in the chapter. You will be asked to explore where you are and where you want to go or what you must do to make your life a LIVINGtouch now. You may even be nudged to change. The questions and activities in this section can be used individually or in a group setting.

As you read, you will be challenged to see yourself as a winner. Winners
- make choices,
- recognize their internal world,
- examine their faith and motivation,
- realize their esteem in Christ,
- graciously give away their gifts,
- explore their external world,
- overcome barriers and obstacles,
- set goals,
- make a commitment to their world,
- take needed action to cross traditional boundaries to reach the unbelieving world for Christ.

Join me in joining God in making a LIVINGtouch!

---

[1]Marsha Spradlin, "My Bold-Witnessing Experience," *Start*, October-November-December 1986, cover 3.

[2]Bill Bright, *Witnessing Without Fear* (San Bernardino: Here's Life Publishers, Inc., 1987), 11.

1
Making Choices

"Then choose for yourself this day whom you will serve" (Josh.
24:15 NIV).

THE TOUCH: THE ENCOUNTER WITH SANDY AND DAVID

Seatbelt buckled. Headphones plugged in. I was anticipating a productive working flight from Birmingham to Ohio where I would lead a two-day seminar on personal witnessing. Such trips were not uncommon. I had been a professional Christian worker for years. Boarding jets, sleeping in motels across the nation, and eating someone else's cooking was a way of life for me.

Normally, I would have been prepared for the seminar I was to lead, but it had been an extremely busy week at the office. I was counting on this travel time to polish my notes for the seminar. I prayed for a quiet spot near the rear of the nonsmoking section. Prayers are not always answered in exactly the way we anticipate.

Just as I prayed for silence I noticed a woman about my age and her son rushing with their boarding passes down the narrow aisle.

"Surely, on a plane as empty as this, these two won't crowd in the seats next to me," I thought.

At that precise moment it happened. The two empty seats next to me were no longer empty. I quickly gathered my papers and notebook from their seats as they squeezed in front of my knees.

1

"Maybe, if I keep my earphones on, they won't talk and I can continue to study."

Wrong again. The plane had hardly started its ascent when the young woman seated next to me thrust her hand into mine.

"Hi, my name is Sandy. This is David, my son. We're on our way to the cold country for a weekend ski trip," she explained.

"Sounds fun to me. I'm Marsha, and I'm on my way to work," I joked, as I managed to explain that I was on my way to a seminar for which I was unprepared, hoping she would take the hint. I simply did not want to be bothered.

Sandy did not take my cue. Instead, within moments her conversation took hold of my heart, mind, and soul. I found myself pulling the earphones out to make sure I was hearing her story correctly.

I could hardly believe what Sandy was telling me. She was obviously hurting. Within the 20-minute flight from Birmingham to Atlanta, Sandy openly shared her pain. Not only had she just experienced a devastating divorce, but only six months earlier she had lost her oldest son as a result of a hunting accident.

As Sandy explained her grief, I began to wonder, "Father, how could anyone endure such pain? How can I possibly share my love, my concern, and my conviction. I have never had such an experience."

I felt frustrated as I felt my own hurt. With all of my training and book knowledge about witnessing and ministering, I had never learned the steps of simply embracing the hurting with His love. After all, Sandy's life-style was so different from my own. Her pain was unlike any pain I had ever experienced. "What do I say?" I prayed frantically.

It was then that I realized it was not me that Sandy should see. She needed to see only the loving embrace of the Father within me that could make the difference. My role was not to take away the pain but to simply be the channel. Yet the choice was still mine. As I listened to this lonely one, I had to ask myself, Do I become a channel to dry her tears and calm her obvious fears? I realized that only in His name could I give hope to her hopelessness and love to her feelings of

2

rejection. In His name I could reach deep within for the right words and expressions.

My heart overflowed with compassion. My mouth became a channel that shared the message of hope to these strangers, who were yet new friends. As I relied totally on the Spirit, I felt His love and compassion flowing through me.

I do not remember what was said during those brief moments. But it was as much what I said as it was the loving acceptance Sandy felt that made the difference. As she shared her grief, His overflow seemed to embrace her. She felt safe, loved, and accepted. Because of feelings of acceptance, Sandy clung to every word of encouragement. As I introduced Sandy to Jesus Christ, by sharing what He had done in my own life, we cried, we prayed, and simply said good-bye, a new sister in Christ.[1]

Choose Whom You Will Serve

While not every contact with a lost or hurting person brings such a spontaneous opportunity to witness, I became deeply convinced that day that a witness from the overflow of God's love is by far the most effective witness. Even more, I realized that such encounters do not just happen. We make the choice to be or not to be the channel. When the emphasis is on being, the doing seems to follow.

What made the difference that day with Sandy and David? As I thought about them all weekend, I remembered the simple analogy of water and steam. At 111°F water is water, but at 112°F water becomes steam. Water has the potential of becoming steam. Unless, however, it is energized through heat, it remains water. The 1 degree makes the difference. What gave me the 1-degree difference that day? I learned that the difference was simply a matter of choice and availability. Only as I chose to merge my heart, mind, and life-style with the Father, did I become an effective witness. The choice was mine!

You make choices every day. Think about this fact. If there is one thing that we should be experts in, it is choice making. How many choices have you already made today? You have chosen what to wear, what to eat, what projects or errands to run, and many other things. Life is choices. If we do not make the choices, someone will usually make them for us. Through choice making we enter the lifelong process of becoming what we will someday be.

I am convinced there are two kinds of Christians. There are Christians who operate from reasons and there are those who operate from results. We either spend all of our time making (choosing) excuses or reasons why we cannot be a personal witness, or we experience the joy of the results of witnessing.

Choice making is like a tightly woven garment with many threads. Each thread is woven into the fabric to strengthen it. The fabric of making choices may have many designs, but the chosen threads are similar. A LIVINGtouch witness makes the choice to be a life-style witness. They choose prayerfully, consciously, willfully, joyfully, ambitiously, and faithfully. Examine each of these choice threads with me.

Prayerfully

An attitude and life-style of being a witness starts in the sanctuary of prayer. It is there we are comforted through faith with the awareness of a power greater than ourselves. Prayer involves faith in God and a belief in His power to change the world through us. It is in this sanctuary of prayer that we not only realize Who God is, but who we are. Likewise, we realize our role in touching the world with Jesus Christ's love.

As we choose to pray, we demonstrate obedience by following His command to pray. It is out of such obedience that a creative and effective witnessing life-style can be molded.

But many of us need help in even wanting to pray. We have somehow developed the conception that prayer is boring. Our motivation to pray seems to spring from oughts and shoulds rather than the genuine desire to be with the Father.

Andrew Murray, a missionary and writer, once wrote about " 'the sin of prayerlessness.' When we do not use our minds to pray, we are being disobedient, self-centered, spiritually weakened, and hindered by Satan."[2]

By saying yes to prayer, we come to know the mind of God. William Carey claimed that "secret, fervent, believing prayer—lies at the root of all personal godliness."[3]

By saying yes to prayer, we grow spiritually and experience the inner joy and peace that comes from moments spent in

4

closeness with the Heavenly Father.

By saying yes to prayer, we learn to serve God more effectively. Strange as it may seem, most of us try to learn such skills in other ways. Bookstore shelves, even Christian ones, are filled with self-help books and programs planned to teach us how to become effective in every area of life. True effectiveness starts when our own creative minds are merged with the Creator's. Yes, I believe in unlimited creative potential, and such creative potential is needed to win the world for Christ. The source of such creative thinking and being, however, is not found through books or tapes, but through the sanctuary of prayer.

By saying yes to prayer, we grow closer to others. Have you ever had a sudden urge to pray for someone? As a result, did you feel closer to that person? As we pray for others we come to know them through the Father's eyes. Prayer is essential in developing the LIVINGtouch life-style.

As I say yes to prayer, I break out of a monologue with myself. My life becomes an unceasing conversation with the Father that is nourished as I experience His life within. This communion with the Father enables Him to manifest Himself in my flesh and everydayness. I become a witness!

Consciously

I am awake from about 5:00 A.M. until 10:00 P.M. Most of that time I would consider myself to be fully alert and capable of making conscious choices. I make hundreds of decisions every day. So do you. But many of these decisions are not as conscious as we might think. How often do you do things automatically?

Each morning, before I am fully awake, I automatically walk to the coffeepot. I do not even have to think about it. I am programmed, I guess. The same automatic pattern is true for driving to work or to the airport. It is as if my car is on autopilot. I do not feel that I consciously think where to turn or when to stop. But that has not always been true. When I first moved to Birmingham I had to think every time I got into my car, "Now, where is the grocery store, the post office, my house?" After a while the routine became easy, and this assurance lessened my need for using as much mental energy. I never think about directions now. When I need groceries I simply go to the same store and usually buy the same things. It is not really a rut, it's my life-style.

Could it be that witnessing could take on some of those similar patterns? At first, witnessing is an effort, a conscious choice. But after a while, it becomes natural and automatic.

Experts in behavioral science agree that we usually do or become that which we think about most often. We control our thoughts every day. Perhaps that is why the Bible stresses, "Whatever is true, whatever is noble, whatever is admirable—anything that is excellent or praiseworthy—think about such things" (Phil. 4:8 NIV).

Becoming a witness must be a conscious choice. As we make the decision to become a witness, we are thinking. We are making a conscious choice.

I have a friend who recently made that choice. In the past several weeks she has made the comment often that everything she picks up to read seems to "zap" her. "Every Scripture verse and book seems to say something about why I should and how I can become an effective witness now!" she explained.

I have a feeling that what my friend is reading is an outgrowth of her conscious choice to become a witness. Her choice has made her more sensitive and selective in what she thinks about and what she reads.

Making a conscious choice to become a witness means choosing to become the kind of person God wants us to be. The choice is a willingness to be molded and changed into His image. "We are the children of God," John wrote in his first epistle. "What we will be has not yet been made known. But we know that when He appears, we shall be like Him."

We can consciously choose to become witnesses. But unless we are willing to let our life-styles merge with His, our choice is in vain. This is where the matter of the two wills come in—my will and His.

Willfully

The thread of the will is woven tightly with the thread of conscious choice making. In fact, the two are so tightly woven that they may appear the same. Yet there are qualities of the willful choice that are unlike those discussed above.

6

A year ago I was speaking at a women's retreat in the East. After the evening meal, I decided to go on a short walk to clear my mind and simply be with the Father alone. While walking in the woods I noticed a most interesting phenomenon. I had seen this scene many times before but had never *really* seen it. I watched an army of ants march smartly in line, each carrying a load of something toward a mound of dirt. They were building their winter home and storing food. I shall never forget my exact thought, "Somebody besides me is in charge here."

As I stood and watched in amazement these tiny creatures marched to the beat of another drummer. I was reminded of the verses in Proverbs, "Take a lesson from the ants, you lazy fellow. Learn from their ways and be wise! For though they have no king to make them work, yet they labor hard all summer, gathering food for the winter. But you—all you do is sleep. When will you wake up? 'Let me sleep a little longer!' Sure, just a little more! And as you sleep, poverty creeps upon you like a robber and destroys you; want attacks you in full armor" (Prov. 6:6-11 TLB).

Yes, someone bigger than me is in charge of the ants. Albert Einstein recognized this fact when he said that the universe operated at the will of a power far superior to mankind—a power before which we should feel humble.

What a relief it was to recognize that I am not in charge of everything. There is a will bigger than my own—God's will. And He is in charge of it all. He simply calls me to the cause.

God is in control and He does have a will. How we fit and merge into this will becomes the matter of choice.

Let us look at God's will first.

Each of us would agree that being a witness means living in the will of God. But what does living in the will of God mean? And how does one accomplish that? We do not accomplish it with our minds, but with our hearts. To one dedicated to the Father, doing His will becomes a natural part of life.

How are we going to find this will? Christian author Oswald Chambers insists that God will not necessarily communicate His will to us. To discover God's will, we must renew our minds and study and obey His word. As we take steps to learn His will, we are overcome with joy because we realize we love to do God's will and doing it comes naturally, freely.

I know of no more humbling truth than to realize that a sovereign God has ordained me to participate in His will. But I must choose.

We have recognized that saying yes to God's will is saying yes to a disciplined life that has a quality to affect the world for Christ. Where does God's will and my will merge? First, we must always remember there are two free wills operating. If we place importance only in the will of God, we lose our sense of responsibility and feel everything is up to God.

But if we place importance only in our will, we take all responsibility upon ourselves and deny God His rightful place as God. Either way God's will is not implemented, and we lose both our joy and our freedom which we found in following His will.

God's Word reminds us through illustrations that God has arranged things in such a way that His action is to be coupled with our action. We see this as we examine how our Father chose to use sinful and weak men and women to accomplish His perfect purpose. God actually allowed these persons the dignity to choose willfully to be a part of what He was doing.

We have that same choice today. That is humbling! That is also faith. To choose to allow God to work through me, I exercise faith. Exercising my faith provides one of the greatest joys of the Christian experience. Someone bigger than myself is in charge. What a relief! What a joy! Being a witness does not have to become an ought or a should. It becomes a joy as my will is merged with His.

Joyfully

What is joy? Is it the same as happiness? How does my joy influence my winning witness?

Think about the person you most enjoy being with. As I think I can call to mind more than one person. While each one is different, there is one quality that is consistent. Each is joyful. Joy is contagious. We are attracted to joyful people. When I have had a no good, very bad day, the last person I prefer to be with is what has been called a NIOP. These persons are those who have a Negative Influence on People. Their every action is the antithesis of joy.

8

The Bible speaks plentifully about joy, but strangely enough, nowhere does it speak about a "happy" Christian. We all know that happiness and joy are not synonyms. Remember, Jesus had joy, and He prayed "that they might have My joy fulfilled in themselves."

I once heard that joy is not something that is to be sought after, but is something that is experienced only in the moment. I believe that is true. Joy is not a destination, nor is it something to be sought. Instead, joy is in the journey. We experience joy as we become rightly related to God.

This truth is in such opposition to the world's view of joy. Let me challenge you to observe the number of messages, commercials, and advertisement campaigns that insist joy can be bought. The secular view of a joyful life insists that joy comes through possessions. Therefore, it is the world's goal and determination to make us as unjoyful as possible so we will seek more possessions. We are bombarded daily with messages that insist that we are living lives of lack and limitation. The message is clear: If we only had a particular brand, product, or possession, we would be joyful.

I must admit that I too fight daily this secular concept of joy. I get caught up in the "someday I'll have" or "someday I'll be" mind-set. When I concentrate on the someday, I lose sight of the now. Joy can only be experienced in the now!

Several years ago I lived on the north side of Dallas, Texas. Today we would call this area the yuppie community. Yuppies have been described as those who have high-tech equipment, computers, videocassette recorders, and microwaves, intermingled with valuable antiques displayed throughout their homes. Most yuppies drive BMWs, wear 100 percent cotton starched shirts, and live in patio homes with neatly manicured lawns. While I did not have a BMW or a patio home, I must admit that I did on occasion drop by the BMW dealership near my third-floor condominium. My definition of joy began to get blown out of proportion. In retrospect, I realize there is nothing wrong with having things. But when things become a vehicle to obtain joy, we are on the road to becoming a losing witness.

Joy is deeper than what I have or what I wear. It is a life-style consistent with the life-style of Jesus Christ. The joy of Jesus was His absolute self-surrender and self-sacrifice to the will of His Father, the joy of doing exactly what the Father sent Him to do. Once again we see threads tightly woven, the thread of joy and the thread of will.

Joy comes with a life that is merged with God and in God and for God! Our goal should not be joy, or peace, or blessing, but God alone! Joy is the stronghold of our Christian faith. It is the miracle of the Christian life. Such miracles can be seen when we experience joy in the midst of external misery.

A while back I received the devastating news that my father had had a severe stroke. Within hours I was on a plane to Mobile, Alabama, to join my family in a crisis unlike any that we had ever experienced. When I arrived I was greeted by at least 50 friends—friends of Dad's who had come to the hospital to support, encourage, and join us in our pain. Dad was in surgery for nearly five hours. We had been told he had a 50 percent chance to live through surgery. He made it through surgery. It was then we learned that he might never regain consciousness, and, if he did, he might never know us. The news was hard to hear and comprehend.

At 2:00 the following morning my mother, sister, sister-in-law, and I walked to the car. We decided to put Dad in God's hands for the rest of the night. My brother stayed the night in the hospital while we went home for a few hours of much needed sleep. I shall never forget Mother's comment as we walked arm in arm to the car, "I can't believe I am leaving my husband in this hospital. I am going home to sleep. Why do I feel so relaxed and at peace? I should be in misery."

My sister-in-law quickly responded, "Wanda, the miracle of real joy comes in the midst of the storm. Remember the people who greeted us and held our hands during those hours of surgery. God is simply answering their prayers to grant us peace and joy in the midst of our misery." Dad did regain consciousness after a six-week coma. He is a walking testimony of the joy that comes through faith in the midst of the storm.

How do we obtain such joy—the kind that is so contagious? Such joy comes only when we allow God to fulfill His design in and through us. Joy, therefore, lies in fulfilling God's purpose for creating us. We fulfill this design when we are at one with the Father. It is then that the Spirit of God fills us and gives us that overflowing sense of joy. Joy is the result

10

of being what we were created for—a witness. It has nothing to do with what is happening around us. Joy is literally the nature of God in me. It is in this environment that we find true energy for being a witness. It is here that others notice a valuable difference in our lives.

Joy is not something to be sought ambitiously, but peacefully, as we become one with the Father.

Ambitiously

A LIVINGtouch witness also needs ambition in order to make choices. I heard a story of an Indian who found an eagle's egg and put it into the nest of a prairie chicken. The eaglet hatched with the brood of chicks and grew up with them. You can imagine the result. The eagle grew up thinking he was a chicken. He never realized he could fly. One day he saw a magnificent bird far above him in the cloudless sky. The beautiful bird soared gracefully on the powerful wind current. The tragedy of the story is that the bird never knew that he too was an eagle. He was convinced he could never soar. The eaglet died thinking he was only a prairie chicken.

What a tragedy. Many Christians are living examples of a similar tragedy as they fail to recognize their potential. These impoverished Christians give up the ambition to be the best for Christ. To become a LIVINGtouch witness, we must give up such limited thinking and identify truly who we are as well as Whose we are. We become camouflaged because of what we tell ourselves or what others tell us about ourselves. We become victims of messages from sources other than the Source of our true identity, the Father. Therefore, we give up our ambitious pursuit to become all that the Father has created us to be.

Have you ever found yourself in a situation like the eaglet? You are aware that the Father's design for your life is to be a witness, and you also know that through His power you can be! But you have set self-imposed limitations. Do not feel like the Lone Ranger. It is much easier to think of reasons why you cannot than to pursue results. There are many "I can't" excuses: "Evangelism simply is not my gift"; "I am not the type to witness"; "I don't know a non-Christian"; "God uses me and my gifts in other ways."

Thinking of reasons for your lack and limitation is the "chicken" way out. It takes effort that is sometimes a 180-degree turn around from our current path of thinking and doing to be able to soar with the eagles as an ambitious winner dedicated to making your witness count. Everything truly worthwhile has a price. Becoming a witness is not excluded from heavy effort. It takes time to become a witness . . . time in prayer, time in study, and time in identifying and getting acquainted with lost persons in your world. The question is: Are you willing to pay the price? Your answer is important, and a no response could cost someone's eternal life.

Faithfully

My ambition to be a witness may be in direct proportion to my willingness to be faithful and consistent in preparing for the witnessing task and in living a consistent Christlike life. A LIVINGtouch witness is one who chooses faithfully every day to celebrate the difference.

Being faithful is a deliberate action of confidence in the character of God. We may not always understand His character, but we can always have faith in Him, no matter how things look.

The important point in faithfulness is that the Father is consistent even though we may not understand or see His consistency. Likewise, to be a witness we must live a lifestyle that is consistent and free of camouflage.

I learned about camouflage through my nephew Justin. It was Christmas Eve. As is the custom of our family, we gathered in the living room to enjoy a family celebration. The hour was very late. My brother excused himself to put two-year-old Justin in bed. As we overheard the conversation between Larry and Justin, we made mental note of Larry's final instructions to his young son: "Justin, I had better not see you out of that bed." Larry rejoined the adult family members as we discussed how long it would be until Justin thought of a legitimate excuse to get out of bed. After five or ten minutes, Justin walked bravely into the middle of the living room and announced, "Daddy, this is not me you see."

Justin's clever and creative technique to camouflage himself worked. For several moments we were laughing so hard we could not see anything. Justin's imagination had defined what was real. By changing his perspective of himself, he was convinced he could also change our perspectives. This experience, hilarious as it was, made me consider deeply the implications of camouflage. How often have I failed to make Christ known because of my own camouflage? To become a witness, one that truly touches lives, I must obtain a life-style free from camouflage and consistent with the life-style of Jesus Christ.

THE CHALLENGE TO TOUCH

How can Christians make a LIVINGtouch difference? How can each believer celebrate a life-style that counts?

A witness starts in making a conscious choice. You have the opportunity to choose this day whom you will serve. You can choose to be a witness.

List below the positive changes that will occur in your witness today as result of this choice. In addition to this foundational decision to be a witness, consider specific ways you can celebrate a life-style that counts.

Read the questions below. Make notes in the space provided for your answers. The choices you make may not only change your life-style but may influence change in someone else's life!

Feel free to review pages 3-13 as you consider answers to these questions:

1. Who will I serve today?

2. What choices will I prayerfully make today?

3. What choices will I consciously make today?

4. What choices will I willfully make today?

5. What choices will I joyfully make today?

13

6. What choices will I ambitiously make today?

7. What choices will I faithfully make today?

8. List the results or impact your choices could have on the lives of someone you know.

---
[1]Marsha Spradlin, "Laser," *Contempo*, February 1987, 41.
[2]Gary R. Collins, *The Magnificent Mind* (Grand Rapids: Baker Book House, 1985), 212.
[3]Ibid., 213.

2
Becoming Aware of Your Internal World

"Search me, O God, and know my heart; test me and know my anxious thoughts. See if there is any offensive way in me, and lead me in the way everlasting" (Psalm 139:1-4; 22-24 NIV).

THE TOUCH: THE ENCOUNTER WITH MYSELF

As the children's book said, it was truly a horrible, terrible, very bad, no good sort of day. Everything that could go wrong did and at the worst possible moment. Any positive witness that counted that day was merely incidental. It was the day I stumbled into myself.

If confession is good for the soul, consider my soul in good shape. However, on that particular day, nothing, in my opinion, felt good, looked good, or even happened that was good.

It all started on the coldest morning of the year. I had an early morning meeting at the office. Normally, I am a morning person, but perhaps I stayed up too late the night before. My subconscious must have heard the alarm go off. When I was finally awake, I found the clock tucked under the cover next to my body in my warm bed. As soon as I realized the time, I jumped up and quickly grabbed the only clean shirt I had starched and ironed. I headed for the shower.

It was there that the already late start got even later. Because of my hurried state of mind, I forgot to properly adjust the water temperature in the shower. The moment I jumped in

I scalded my head. Jumping out of the shower quickly was not a smart move. It resulted in an incredible slide across the cold tiled bathroom floor. My head hit first.

I quickly convinced myself that I did not have time for head injuries. So I readjusted the water and started over, this time to be greeted with an eyeful of shampoo. As I reached for the towel, I missed. Remember the only starched shirt I had to wear? How could I tell it wasn't the towel? After all, both eyes were glued shut.

The shower experience was enough to cause anyone's day to get started with a literal bang! Bad became worse when my contact lens decided to reside permanently in the sink drain rather than my left eye.

"There's no time for breakfast, much less quiet time," I thought.

Dressed, with one contact lens, a wet shirt, a bruised head, and wounded spirit, I grabbed my keys, coat, and briefcase and rushed to the car.

"Perfect," I thought as I got a runner in my stockings somehow from scraping ice from the windshield. "Never mind. I have a meeting in three minutes," I thought frantically.

My driving speed was intense. So was the police officer's voice who pulled me over for speeding. Why he didn't give me a ticket, I will never know. Maybe it was the wet shirt and obvious lack of a contact lens that did it. It certainly was not my charming personality.

I made it to the office only eight minutes late. When I entered the room where the meeting was to be held, I felt I had blown it again. "Where is everyone?"

The meeting had been cancelled!

I was not a happy person. I was mad, hungry, hurting, spiritually malfunctioning, and depressed. How I felt about myself was obvious, not only to me, but to everyone else, it seemed. The day was declared, "Be nice to Marsha day. She's a little on edge."

My inner feelings of lack and limitation seemed to be reflected in everything I did. I felt horrible about myself, and likewise about everyone else.

I did learn something from the experience. When my inner world is in shambles, my external world reflects that state of being. When I feel poorly about who I am, I lack the ability to communicate anything positive about Who He is. I am thankful for forgiveness, for second chances, for the opportunity to learn and grow, and for a Father Whose love for me is unconditional.

Where does one receive and nurture the inner Source that provides stamina, positive determination, and the unswerving ability to look consistently at events in a different way? Can we really have spiritual solitude on such stormy days?

Recognize Your Internal World

What is the inner world, and why is it so significant in making a winning witness?

The inner world makes up our spiritual, emotional, mental, and physical self. "Here is a center in which choices and values can be determined, where solitude and reflection might be pursued," said author Gordon MacDonald.[1]

Self-discovery may be one of the most exciting experiences in life. Likewise, it can become one of the great battlegrounds of life. There seems to be a contest that must be fought. Since our public (outer) world is so filled with what seem to be infinite demands of time, loyalties, money, and energy, our inner worlds often suffer. The battle comes as we struggle to keep a balance. The outer world usually screams the loudest for our attention.

None of us are free from a demanding outer world. We each share massive responsibilities at home, at work, as well as at church. We have become convinced that good people work hard and are very tired! Therefore, we tend to try to live up to being good people by taking on more responsibility than we can handle. It is like juggling balls; one ball must be dropped in order to pick up another.

I too suffer from an imbalanced attention to my inner world. My life often becomes so heavy with surface responsibilities that both worlds—the inner and outer—suffer fatigue, disillusionment, and sometimes defeat.

What causes our inner world to so often experience neglect? And what can we do to quieten the well-meaning noise making such demands of us?

It is comforting to know that there is an inner world beneath the surface noise and action. This inner world needs to be explored and maintained in order to gain the strength and resilience to bear the pressures of our everyday life. If my inner world is to be maintained, it is because I have made a choice to monitor it every day. Without such attention, my effectiveness as a witness will be denied. What will turn the tide for making the inner world a priority? First, spiritual orderliness.

• Spiritual orderliness. Orderliness inside for the Christian first comes as we are related rightly to the Father.

While I am a firm believer in daily devotional time in prayer and meditation, I also feel that spiritual orderliness must go deeper than the number of minutes spent with God. The emphasis should be on the quality of time spent with the Father. Gordon MacDonald believes that if the private world is in order, it is because one has chosen for the inner world to rule the outer world.

Without a constant abiding relationship with Him, how can I expect to recognize the world of lost, hurting, and hungry people? How can I know how to minister and witness? It is in the spiritual sanctuary of my life that I can in quietness reflect upon my values. There I can be free to worship God without the outer world intruding.

Spiritual growth is not a one-time project. It is a neverending awareness of our failure to live up to our life in Christ. It is a lifelong attempt to be true to ourselves and live up to that life. Growing spiritually is a deliberate and disciplined choice that we must make. Even though such growth may be painful at times, it is necessary to experience the reestablishment of the Christ-centered life at the deepest level. Growth often means an opening within our deepest self to see the light of God. Nothing is going to satisfy the deepest internal, spiritual need until we have fellowship with Him. Fellowship with the Father will in turn result in fellowship with others.

• Emotional orderliness. It is hard to separate the emotional world from the spiritual one. They are so tightly woven that one seems to govern the other. When the spiritual world is in order, the emotional realm of our inner selves is usually in order too.

What are emotions? It may be easier to describe them than to define them. We each experience a variety of emotions every day: joy, anger, depression, liberation, anxiety, and even fear. Emotions could be defined as the mind's interpretation of something. This interpretation can be real or unreal. One's perception of the event is what dictates the emotion. Anger, joy, depression, and freedom are emotional ways of thinking. These emotions usually begin when some event occurs or some idea enters one's thinking.

I have found that most Christians are uncomfortable even discussing their real emotions. Deep within, I think we each feel we are a little artificial and neurotic. Or maybe we think all the world is a little peculiar except for us.

How do we as Christians deal with the emotional aspects of our inner worlds? First, we must recognize that life without emotions would be dull. Emotions are not bad, but an inappropriate perspective and response to an emotion can be devastating to our witness.

In his book *The Magnificent Mind*, Gary Collins interprets the way emotions operate within all of us. Examine his illustration:

EVENT OR IDEA

INTERPRETATION: We find meaning
in the event or idea

EMOTION: This is a response
to the interpretation

REACTION to the emotion[2]

Emotions are healthy and a part of daily life. As Christians, we must base our confidence in God and His grace. By doing so, our emotional responses become the most beautiful design of our lives, not the source of life.

Accepting our emotions is a wholesome part of God's economy. When we accept the way we are, that acceptance better enables us to come to the Cross, die to self and what is ours, and let Him be Lord.

• Mental orderliness. We have already discovered that emotions usually hinge on a mental interpretation. Our mental inner world is tightly woven to emotions. As Christians, what role should the mind play in the inner world?

Did you know that there are approximately 200 biblical references to the word *mind?* As Christians, we are given instructions for mind development.

> "Finally, brothers, whatever is true, whatever is noble, whatever is right, whatever is pure, whatever is lovely, whatever is admirable—if anything is excellent or praiseworthy—think about such things" (Phil. 4:8 NIV).

We have been given promises as people whose minds are focused on spiritual issues. Isaiah states that we will experience perfect peace if we put our trust in God and let our minds think about Him.

In several places the Scriptures challenge us to work together united "with one mind." Imagine what would happen if all Christians worked together, with one mind, to win the lost world to Christ!

The Bible also instructs us to have the mind of Christ. "For who has known the mind of the Lord that he may instruct him? But we have the mind of Christ" (1 Cor. 2:16).

As Christians, we are expected to develop our inner mental world by developing the mind of Christ. We are expected to think like Christ. Thus, the logical next question is this one: What did He think about?

First, Christ thought about and knew the Scriptures. He was constantly aware of the Father and sensitive to the guidance of the Holy Spirit.

Second, Jesus demonstrated a caring mind. As He gave instructions to His disciples, Jesus stated repeatedly that the greatest characteristic of a Christian must be love.

Third, He had a heavenly mind. Paul instructed Christians to "set our minds on things above, not on earthly things" (Col. 3:2).

And, fourth, Jesus demonstrated an obedient mind. He submitted His will to that of the Father. "When Christ came into the world he said: . . . I have come to do your will, O God" (Heb. 10:7 NIV).

Taking on the characteristics of Christ's mind results in

strong mental effort—thinking clearly, confidently, and courageously. Otherwise, our minds can easily be taken hostage by stagnation or the mind-set of the world. Developing the mind-set of Christ is not a once-and-for-all experience. It is daily. When people stop learning, they stagnate. Renewing the mind daily is the only way to stay healthy. It takes discipline to develop the mind-set of Christ. Oswald Chambers insists that "it is impossible to be of any use to God if we are lazy."[3]

Alert Christ-mindedness means disciplining our thoughts. Why? We do become what we think about. Do you really want to be a LIVINGtouch witness? Then think about it, read about it, saturate yourself in experiences and situations where your mind can be filled with examples of what it means to live a life that celebrates the difference.

• Physical orderliness. Somehow I am not surprised by Joseph Aldrich's description of effective evangelism. "God's strategy for evangelism involves a beautiful bride. . . . A bride is the epitome of all that is right and beautiful. She's a symbol of purity, hope, purpose, trust, love, beauty, and wholeness in a world pockmarked with ugliness."[4]

What does such an illustration have to do with the physical body? Simply this: the beauty and graceful charisma that the winning Christian life-style exhibits is more attractive when housed in a body that is truly God's temple. But, all too often, the physical appearance is the last area to be discussed or even thought about in personal evangelism. Why should it matter what I look like if my heart is right? Should that not be enough?

No! I am convinced that an effective witness is one that takes every effort to make his or her body fit and attractive physically. This statement does not mean that only those with perfect bodies make an impact on the world for Christ. It does mean, however, that persons who give proper attention to their bodies are leading disciplined life-styles that will yield not only physical stamina, but attract men and women to Christ.

Have you ever noticed the number of passages in both the Old and New Testaments that discuss the body? Take a moment to rediscover some of these passages: Genesis 1:27, Psalm 139:14, 1 Corinthian 6:19, 1 Timothy 4:14, Romans 12:1, and 3 John 2. God expects everyone to be spiritually and physically fit!

I am convinced that self-confidence, esteem, and even our emotional and spiritual outlooks on life are reflected in both the way we treat our bodies as well as the way we dress, eat, and act. Think about it. We will deal more with the body and how it relates to self-esteem in chapter 4.

Balance is the key to the inner world. We must work to keep the physical appearance attractive, yet remember that what is inside us is even more important. God wants us to have healthy thoughts and motives, as well as healthy food and exercise.

As we maintain order inside our inner worlds, we are prepared to be witnesses in the outer world. The LIVINGtouch witness makes development and maintenance of this inner world the highest priority. If the inner world is not secure and highly maintained, it is in jeopardy of being influenced by the outside. Are we going to secure our inner world so that it will have an influence on the outer world? Or will we neglect this private part of our lives and permit the outer world to shape us? This choice must be made daily in the quiet places of the inner world, from which order and energy come. Then we can overcome the turbulence and influence the outer world for Jesus Christ.

It is there, the inner world, that we shall examine now. Have you been plagued with fear, lack of awareness, excuses or lack of ability, or refusal to be available? Inner solitude can only begin when we are willing to be honest with ourselves.

If I could live that horrible, terrible, very bad, no good sort of day over, could I have done something to make it different? Perhaps the answer is yes and no.

The events may have been the same, but the way I chose to handle them could have been significantly different. The difference, which could have resulted in a LIVINGtouch encounter, could have been my perception and interpretation of the events. Had I had the balanced, internal solitude that holds life together, my view of the annoying events could have been obviously different. The result could have touched someone's heart for Christ.

THE CHALLENGE TO TOUCH

Is your inner world getting slighted because of the constant demands from the outer world? Think specifically about four dimensions of your life: spiritual, emotional, mental, and physical. In the space below, rate your condition on a scale from 1 to 5. (Five being excellent, 3 average, and 1 not in good shape.) Underneath your rating, write a sentence to explain your answer. Next, think about what you will do today to improve and nurture your inner world. Write your answer underneath the "I Will" column. Finally, what impact can your inner solitude have on someone's life for Jesus Christ? Write your answer underneath the "Impact" column.

A Spiritual Climate Check

Dimensions	Today's Condition	I Will	Impact
Spiritual	1-2-3-4-5		
Emotional	1-2-3-4-5		
Mental	1-2-3-4-5		
Physical	1-2-3-4-5		

[1]Gordon MacDonald, *Ordering Your Private World* (Nashville: Oliver-Nelson, 1985), 14.

[2]Gary R. Collins, *The Magnificent Mind* (Grand Rapids: Baker Book House, 1985), 76. Used by permission.

[3]Oswald Chambers, *Oswald Chambers: The Best from All His Books* (Nashville: Thomas Nelson Inc., Publishers, 1987), 213.

[4]Joseph C. Aldrich, *Life-style Evangelism* (Portland: Multnomah Press, 1981), 25.

3
Examining Your Faith—the Key to a LIVINGtouch

"I tell you the truth, if you have faith as small as a mustard seed, you can say to this mountain, 'Move from here to there' and it will move. Nothing will be impossible for you" (Matt. 17:20-21 NIV).

THE TOUCH: THE ENCOUNTER WITH ANDREA

"Who is she?" I wondered. "She has certainly blended in with the crowd.

"There is nothing unusual about her. She is cute, tiny, and quiet," I thought as I stood in the breakfast line on the second morning of the retreat. She was standing close behind me.

I wanted to talk with her, but I was afraid speaking even one word to her would scare her away. Yet, I sensed she wanted to know me. This wasn't the first time I had noticed her nearby.

Just the day before I observed that each time I got up for coffee refills, she got up for coffee refills. When I took my plate to the counter, she took her plate to the counter. But she sat on the back row of each session and said nothing.

Breakfast was over. I decided to get one last cup of coffee before going to my conference room. That is when it happened. With hot coffee in my hand, I turned around too quickly. We indeed had an encounter! My mysterious friend was standing too close behind me.

"I'm sorry. I think I've just poured coffee all over that pretty sweater. Let me get some napkins and help you get cleaned up. I feel just awful!"

"Oh, it's OK . . . really. This is an old sweater anyway," she replied.

I could not believe it. This quiet little one could speak!

"My name is Marsha and I've been wanting to meet you, but certainly not this way," I said.

"I've wanted to meet you too, but I was kind of afraid to just come up and talk to you."

"Afraid! Ha! Come on. Let me get us both a second cup of coffee and let's visit. I have five minutes before the session. I just wish we had done this sooner. My plane leaves right after lunch today. We can visit fast!" I urged.

Andrea and I sat in a corner away from the crowd. I sensed a troubled young woman wanting attention. I was right.

Five minutes was not long enough. It was enough time, however, to find out how deeply troubled this 17-year-old girl was.

"I'm not supposed to be here," she said.

"What do you mean, Andrea?"

"I am not like all of these other nice girls. I am supposed to be in jail this weekend, but when I told the judge I was going to a Christian retreat, he decided that this might be better for me than jail. After all, I've been there more times than most people go to the grocery store."

What I heard and what I saw did not match. Was this cute, bashful, innocent teenager a criminal?

"I've listened to what you've said about God and all. It sounds real interesting, but it couldn't work for me. I could never be that good. You see, you have no idea how bad I am. I have been in drugs, theft, I have been raped, name it. I have either done it or had it done to me. How could God ever want anyone like me?"

"Wait. Andrea, who said anything about having to be good? Being good has nothing to do with accepting Christ. We accept Christ first of all because He is good, loving, and forgiving; and second because we aren't good. If I had waited until I was 'good enough' I would still not know Him personally. The good comes later, and even then we Christians still make many mistakes."

25

I could tell there was a lot of territory that needed to be covered, but I had to go. I had a seminar.

"Andrea, will you come to my seminar? Maybe we can squeeze in a couple of minutes afterwards."

"Absolutely not!"

I would have felt rejected, but I did not have time.

As soon as I got to my session she was there, sitting on the back row. As I spoke, I could not help but think about our conversation. There were at least 30 women in the room; yet, I found myself speaking to Andrea. When the conference was over, she was the last to leave.

"I have got to run up the hill to the dorm and pack. Why don't you go with me? We can finish our visit."

"Absolutely not!" she insisted.

I had no choice. I had to go.

Only a moment had passed. I had only had time to put my suitcase on the bed when I heard a knock on my door. It was Andrea.

"Get in here! It's freezing outside," I said.

I found myself making conversation, hoping she would say something in response that would give me a clue as to how I could minister and share my faith.

She said nothing.

I knew I had ten minutes before the retreat coordinator would blow her car horn to signal that she was ready to shuttle me off to the airport. I felt I had no other choice. I had to talk fast and trust that the Father would interpret my words and touch her heart.

"Andrea, I am not sure why the judge let you off. But I am sure glad you are here. Let me tell you why."

During the next five or six minutes I shared the depths of my heart. I said things that ordinarily I would have reserved for close friends. I simply wanted to communicate quickly my genuine love and concern for her. I knew I might never have such an opportunity again. I shared what Jesus Christ had done in my life, the miracles He had performed. I shared God's plan of salvation and then said: "Andrea, will you trust Him? Will you simply let Him inside to love you?"

"No way! Absolutely not!"

I felt rejected. I felt I had just shared every ounce of love, wisdom, and "guts" I had. Then suddenly I realized it was

26

not me whom she was rejecting. She was rejecting the Father. I closed the suitcase. The car horn was blowing. I rushed to the door. "Just a minute. One more minute." Closing the door, I quickly opened my briefcase. Inside was one of the magazines my company publishes. My name, address, and telephone number were printed inside the cover. "Andrea, will you write me?" "Yea! Maybe I will." "Andrea, can I pray . . . right now before I leave?" "I don't care. If it would make you feel better," she replied apathetically. Reaching out to embrace her, I prayed. I wept. She simply stood there like a cold statue exhibiting no emotions. Afterward, I said, "I love you!"

Staring at the cold wooden floor, Andrea said, "Have you ever felt that you just met your best friend, and now she is going away?" Ah! There was the first sign of hope. "One day, Andrea, we will talk again." I wanted to give her something.

Spontaneously, I pulled off my name tag that was stuck to my coat and put it on her sweater. "This is so you won't forget that someone loves you."

Andrea removed her name tag and stuck it on my coat. "This is so you will not forget to pray for me."

The horn was blowing. I hugged Andrea and together we rushed out the door. It was snowing. Beautiful! The conference coordinator had a camera. Quickly she jumped out of the car and took our picture. Andrea and I posed against a tree, arm-in-arm, with each other's name tag temporarily stuck to our clothes.

She had touched my heart like none other. I couldn't stop thinking about her. The flight home was dominated with thoughts about Andrea. "Will I ever hear from her? Will she continue in the drug culture? Who can I contact that can follow up?"

Monday morning seemed to come earlier than usual. The retreat had wiped me out. But I was at the office at 7:30. The phone was ringing the moment I walked into my office.

I dropped my briefcase on the floor and in my professional voice said, "This is Marsha Spradlin."

"Marsha, this is Andrea."

That phone call was the first of a series of calls, not to mention the volumes of letters and cards, from Andrea over the next several months. In fact, I am sure the US Postal Service opened an extra branch office simply to handle our correspondence. What started as a simple exchange of name tags became a long-term, and sometimes frustrating, commitment of trying to make a winning difference to touch Andrea's life for Jesus Christ.

The months that followed were exhilarating at times, yet frustrating and even fearful on other occasions. Nothing was simple to Andrea. She questioned everything. Her questions led me to examine my own faith, and to even grow with her in her understanding of Who Jesus Christ was and could be in her life.

Many of my well-meaning friends questioned why I would spend so much time corresponding and often enduring the infinite phone calls that came, sometimes in the middle of the night.

"Marsha, you had better be careful. This girl is a drug case. She needs professional help. You can't get involved in the lives of every basket case you stumble into on these trips across the country," one friend explained.

Andrea was a basket case. But the basket was empty. I knew only Jesus could fill it. I also knew I was incompetent for feeding her all she needed. I had no experience in counseling the drug-addicted personality. Even though I read books, talked to friends, and sought professional counsel myself in order to relate to Andrea, I was confident only the Father could teach me how to get through to her.

I remembered the story of the loaves and fishes. I remembered the way Jesus fed the multitudes with only a couple of loaves. I remembered that happened only because of faith and the boy's availability to give all he had. So, I gave to the Father all I had. A typewriter, a telephone, a Bible, and the source of strength through my relationship with the Father!

The first barrier crossed was Andrea's acceptance that I would be her friend. I would not judge her or put her down. I would not allow her to do that to herself either. I knew I had to demonstrate love, unconditionally. This was hard for me. She called often from jail. Her parents even called and asked me to "get out of the picture." They felt Andrea was growing dependent upon me. They were right.

How could I help her to switch that dependence from me to the Father? I simply had no answers. I felt torn, and also felt the need to honor her parents' request.

Yet the letters continued to pour in, often three to four a week. These letters were my cue that Andrea was starving for answers. But often I was not sure of her questions.

I began to share my concern for Andrea with my editor and dear friend, Mary Ann. She became my prayer partner and an objective coach. Mary Ann asked if Andrea had a Bible.

"A Bible? Of course, I must send a Bible," I realized.

On her birthday, Andrea received a New Testament.

Inside I placed a card. My note said:

Don't call or write me again until you have read the book of James, and have written down at least three questions regarding the meaning of the verses. I love you, Honey! Happy Birthday. One day you will celebrate another kind of birthday. I know that for sure. There are too many people who are praying for you.

Love, Marsha

Please realize I am not advising anyone to take that type of action. I am not completely sure why I did what I did. Doubts consumed me. Had I blown it? Had I made demands when I should simply be her friend and accept her as she is?

Two weeks passed. I was frantic. Did she get the Bible? Had she taken an overdose? Was she in jail? Where was that kid?

The phone did not ring. But finally a letter came. No, it was an epistle. In the letter were at least 15 questions from the book of James. Have you ever tried to answer questions from the book of James?

I called in my prayer partner, Mary Ann. We took the questions and jotted down answers. Neither of us were theologians, but we were Christians and believed in the priesthood of the believer, so we saturated each question with prayer.

I typed out a letter with our interpretation of answers to Andrea's questions. With it, I gave her another reading assignment. John! All of it!

29

Within a week I received the first telephone call in over a month.

"Marsha, I am in jail. It's OK. I didn't do it. My friends had drugs. I was with them so we are all four in the slammer; but I have my letter and my Bible. I also got a notebook from the police lady here. I am reading John and writing my questions. Pray for me."

Mary Ann and I met in the office prayer room for over an hour. We prayed.

The letters continued to come in. For the next several months Andrea struggled with drugs to the point that she was finally placed in a drug rehabilitation center. But not by her choice. She wrote from the center:

Dear Big Sis:
How can I ever have peace without God by my side? I will always carry scars inside of me from the things that have happened to me. How can I forgive and forget? I can't. Do you understand that? I have had more things happen to me than most people go through in a lifetime. God didn't help me then. Why should I believe He will now?
Andrea

One month later:
Dear Sis:
Do you really have to be a Christian to go to heaven? I don't understand why God has to play such an important part of your life.
Andrea

Two weeks later:
Dear Sis:
Someday I might become your sister in Christ. For now, I hope you will understand that I am very scared to turn my life over to Jesus Christ. I have never relied on anyone before. I think my biggest problem is that I have been through a lot and have dealt with everything by myself just fine. So, why do I need Jesus?
Andrea

Later:
Dear Sis:
I am doing fine at the rehabilitation center. I am getting a promotion. I am getting out and will have to come back only twice a week. Mrs. Jackson, my counselor, said if I am really good I can be a group leader. I guess I have learned that I was more

addicted than I realized. Oh, I went to a revival. I had to dust off your Bible. People stared at me. No one could believe it was me.

Andrea

Six weeks later:
Dear Sis:
If I do come to know Jesus, I want you to be there if possible. I am getting better, but think maybe it would be best if Jesus was on my side.

Andrea

Six weeks later the telephone rang. I had been at the office for only a few minutes. It was Andrea.

"Marsha, you won't believe what happened! I just couldn't stand it any longer."

Fear entered my mind. "Oh no, she's back in jail or on drugs." She had made such progress. I felt she was getting so close to making a real change.

"Marsha, I called the preacher at 4:00 A.M. I told him I had to become a Christian. He met me at his office. I accepted Jesus Christ. He told me everything to do. I knew already. You had told me, but I thought since I had gotten him out of bed, I could at least let him run through it. We're sisters, really sisters, and I love you!"

I could not speak. She had never said, "I love you." And, yes, finally we were sisters. The months of going on faith suddenly turned into reality. My little sister Andrea was now a Christian.

Andrea finished high school and entered college. She married a bright, Christian young man. They live in Maine and are both active members of their church. Their marriage is a beautiful friendship. Each is committed to making a difference in someone's life.

I still get cards and occasional telephone calls, but her dependence is on the Father now, not me. My experience with Andrea taught me about faith, unconditional love, and acceptance. She touched my life.

Why Do I Believe?

I recall as a young person being asked a question about my faith: If you were accused of believing in Jesus Christ, would

31

there be enough evidence to convict you?

While I have heard that question many times since then, I have continued to feel it to be a valid question regarding a self-examination of my own faith.

Why do I believe what I believe? Is it because my belief was handed down to me from my parents, upbringing, etc? Or is it because of a personal relationship that is far easier to describe than to define? Perhaps it is impossible to state explicitly in words what faith is. If we could, then what we are trying to express may not be faith.

There are several basic questions that must be covered in a quality examination. These are the same questions used often as a jury attempts to convict someone of a crime. These questions are the foundation for evidence. They are: What? Why? How? Who? When?

Exploring Our Faith

Faith is obviously important in the Christian life. The word *faith* is listed or referred to in the Bible as much, if not more, than any other verb.

When we talk about faith—and belief—we must do so from the basic assumption that faith is a command, a mandate. "Go thy way; and thou hast believed, so be it done unto thee."

This simple statement actually cuts two ways. It tells us what faith is, the key that can unlock the doors for every believer. It also imprisons those who lack the ability to believe. With faith you can do all things. Yet without it you are locked into your own prison of lack and limitations.

Faith is more than positive or possibility thinking. Faith is "the hope for things unseen." It means giving up everything but belief in God. Faith depends upon God alone. It is neither intellectual belief, emotional desire, or willful decision. It is focus entirely upon God.

Faith is fact. I believe He is!

Faith is mental assessment of the fact. I believe He can. Faith is not a conscious thing. It is a result of our relationship with Him. Faith is resting on the fact. I believe He did. When we say we do not have faith, "we simply betray our own case, that we have no confidence in God at all, for faith is born of confidence in Him."[1]

32

Faith. Why do we need it? Security is a basic need within every one of us. We cannot move from insecurity into security without faith. We all want to be sure of our beliefs, at peace with God, and to get relief from the anxiety that sometimes descends on us.

There is a second reason for needing faith. Without faith we cannot be rightly related to Jesus Christ. It is so simple, yet so profound. Faith does not earn us a relationship with God. It moves us close to God and opens the door for God to reach us.

Third, without faith I can do nothing; but with faith all things are possible. Matthew 17:20 describes faith as a grain of mustard seed. While it is true that such a grain of faith can move a mountain, we must be careful not to confuse faith with a reward system. Faith is not designed simply to enable us to enjoy His blessings.

How do we get faith?

Simply stated, we receive faith from God. However, we are required to take part also. Receiving faith is an act of will, a conscious choice of acceptance. It is not an emotional act, yet emotions certainly follow. Receiving faith is realizing the authority God manifested to meet our needs. The key word is *receiving*.

Another key word in obtaining faith is *resting*. We all want somewhere to rest our hearts and minds. Faith is the only place to rest and the only way to come to God. Faith is not resting in prior experiences. We are to rest only in the Lord. Resting includes being content. Read Philippians 4:12-13. We learn from the verses how to live a life of contentment in every situation when we have faith.

We get faith by receiving and resting, but there is more. *Acting* upon our faith is also key. Faith without action is nothing. There is, therefore, only one way to live the life of faith and that is to live it! It results in actions that are consistent and obedient to the Father's will. Such actions include going out and winning the world to Christ.

Perhaps we all get a little tired of those who just sit around wringing their hands and wishing they had more faith, or some faith. Wishing alone will not do it. We must put action to our faith to make it live.

Who receives faith? God is no respecter of persons. Faith is the promise of the realization of things hoped for and unseen. One individual does not have power above another in his or her ability to receive faith. It is available to each of us equally. (We will explore faith as a spiritual gift in chap. 5.) The question is this: Are you willing to receive it? Receiving it means acting on it.

Exercising Your Faith
Have you ever considered how many things get better when you use them? Take your muscles, for example. I remember once having a weeklong virus. It was not the virus that got me. Instead, it was the one week of not using my muscles. My weakness was as much from the inability to move about, as weakness from the virus. Can you lose faith when you do not exercise it? That question is worthy of our consideration.

Faith: When do you recognize and use it?

Faith, as we have already seen, is born when we use it, as we exercise our confidence in God through our actions. The proof that we have a lively faith is that we are acting it out in our lives, and witnessing with our mouths as to how it came about. It is truth becoming reality!

As Christians, we have plenty of times in our lives when we have opportunity to exercise our faith. Consider a few such times.

Deserts. Have you ever been in a desert? The major feature of the desert is its dryness. Such dryness causes us to depend upon external sources of water, sources not within ourselves.

A physics professor once asked this question in a test: If you were on a desert and your car broke down, and you had only one gallon of water, would you sip on it a little at a time or would you drink it all at once? My answer was sip. I was wrong. The answer is drink it all. Then, as your body needs the moisture, it uses it. Meanwhile, the body stores the extra moisture within the body's tissues and releases the moisture at the exact time needed.

We do not always know when we need relief from our dryness. I do not mean to imply that faith can be stored up for a dry day, but I do feel confident that God is the Source. As we drink daily from His living well, He will supply all that we need in the dry periods of doubt, despair, and testing that will surely come—even to Christians.

I am inclined to forsake the desert as much as possible. To me, the desert means pain, suffering, and isolation. It is a hard place to live and grow, both spiritually and physically. Yet our lives are filled with desertlike experiences. These experiences are unavoidable.

I have learned the greatest lessons in my life in the midst of desertlike struggles. It has been there that external noise was quietened so I could listen to God's voice alone and rely on His unlimited resources, even though the living water was not in sight.

Dryness leads to dependence. Life in the desert depends upon the mercy of a gracious God. Only a person who has lived in a spiritual desert knows how to totally rely upon God because He is all that is left.

It is in the desert that we learn the brighter side of life and faith. The desert provides us the opportunity to think clearly. It is there, in the quietness, that the call to be faithful is strengthened.

Clouds are also a good place to exercise faith. Clouds may be those times of sorrow or suffering in our personal lives which may seem to dispute what we think is the "rule" of God. But it is those very clouds that God uses to teach us how to walk by faith. Without clouds, we would have no faith.

Light is also a time to reaffirm our faith. Yes, there is light at the end of the tunnel for those who believe. How often have you prayed, believed, and then, when you least expected it, the light came?

As I reflect on my experience with Andrea, I remember the dryness, the desert, the clouds, but then the light. The light came the moment she called and said, "I couldn't stand it any longer, I am your sister."

But light is not as simple as turning a switch. Light comes in degrees and comes with perspective. For the blind person there is no light, even in the brightest room. So, could there be light, even if and when we do not see it?

Light is there even when we do not see it. Faith is believing light is there even when we are unable to see with our human eyes and hearts.

I have often wondered if seeing is believing or if believing is seeing? Most of my life I thought seeing was believing. Now I know, however, that believing is seeing! I may not know where I am going, but I can be confident about Who is going with me. And, if I am going to go with Him, I often must revise my attitude toward Who He is. I have to see Him and Him alone. Not myself. Not my lack and limitation. And certainly not my fears.

The Scriptures are clear. "Take no thought for your life . . . nor for your body." In other words, I must not think about those things of which I have been thinking—myself.

I used to think if I believed enough, God would tell me where to go, what to do, and so on. Now I know that He will usually not tell me, for telling me only causes me to lose sight of Who He is and therefore redirects my focus back toward myself.

He simply insists I focus on Who He is. Who is He? "I am the light of the world!" Faith is the promise of the realization of things hoped for and unseen. "Faith is not that I see God, but that I know God sees me."[2]

Faith. Where do you get it?

Living faith comes in the everydayness. It may come wrapped in the pain of the desert, or in the clouds, or in the light. It comes as I am obedient to a relationship with Him. It comes through exercise, putting action to my belief even when His command makes no sense to me. Such exercise implies an unusual amount of faith.

Faith is manifested as I express my thankfulness to the Father by giving all of myself over to Him. It is the unbreakable confidence in God over and above everything He may do. It is a life called and set apart.

From where does it come? It comes in and through faithfulness.

THE CHALLENGE TO TOUCH

Do not be afraid to examine your faith. You may be surprised to learn how strong your faith really is. Do a self-examination by reading Hebrews 11 and asking yourself the following six questions.

Exploring Your Faith
Write your answers in the space provided.
- Faith: What is it?

- Faith: Why do I need it?

- Faith: How do I get it?

- Faith: Who receives it?

Exercising Your Faith
- Faith: When do I recognize and use it?

- Faith: Where do I get it?

Write a brief description of the present state of your faith.

How can you activate it more? Ask yourself, prayerfully:
Do I trust You, Lord?

---

[1]Oswald Chambers, *Oswald Chambers: The Best from All His Books* (Nashville: Thomas Nelson Inc., Publishers, 1987), 110.
[2]Ibid., 112.

4
Recognizing Your Esteem Through the Touch of Jesus Christ

"I praise you because I am fearfully and wonderfully made; your works are wonderful, I know that full well" (Psalm 139:14 NIV).

THE TOUCH: AN ENCOUNTER WITH SARAH AND RAMON

Each morning at 6:00 she was there collecting the money and taking the breakfast order for the ranks of the North Dallas white-collar class who found grabbing a bite on the way in to work convenient. At least most of her customers belonged to that group of persons. Not I. I no longer worked. Talk about low self-esteem.

I had been grounded temporarily from work and travel. A prolonged illness resulting in a five-week hospital stay mandated a three-month leave of absence from my job. I was used to the high pressure world where gratification and personal fulfillment were tightly woven with results. My self-esteem had been so closely tied with what I did and how much I produced that I was finding the days of doing nothing extremely painful.

My condominium was small. I spent nearly 24 hours a day there. After only a week or two I began to crave places to spend my time. Early in the furlough I discovered that

McDonald's opened at 6:00 A.M. So I decided to join the breakfast bunch. Soon I began to take my Bible and notebook to read after breakfast. Then I pulled out my old briefcase and began to make up work to do. It was not long until I was spending the entire morning (at least five days a week) with Sarah, Ramon, Bill, Jill, Barb, and the other employees and regular customers at the "Golden Arches."

After a few days I noticed Sarah. She was overweight. Her complexion was scarred, her hair stringy, and she seemed a bit slow mentally. She never looked up when taking orders. She exhibited such low self-esteem.

One morning I was determined to look her in the eyes and say good morning.

"Sarah, it's a great day, isn't it?"

"How did you know my name? No one has ever called me by my name here before," she said.

"Your name tag."

The next morning when I arrived she looked at me.

"Good morning. Coffee?" she asked.

"How did you remember, Sarah?" I asked.

"I've been watching you. Every day you drink coffee and read. We all talk about you. Are you a famous writer or something? After all, you write for hours. We have all decided that maybe you are writing a book!"

"Oh, Sarah, a book! I could write a book. Maybe one day what I write in this white notebook will be a book," I replied.

I began to watch Sarah during the next few days. She spent all of her time, when not behind the counter, sweeping the floor in my area. I always sat in the same place, the corner next to the large front window. My corner stayed spotless.

"You certainly are a hard worker," I said one morning as her broom chased a straw wrapper across the already shiny floor.

"I like things to look good. Say, Ramon, he's the Hispanic guy who washes the windows, wanted me to ask you what you do. I mean, are you married? Do you have a job? He was afraid to ask you himself. He just thinks you are nice and pretty. And, well, you are."

Silently I thought, "pretty." That was the first time some-one had said that in, well, I could not remember when. So much of my self-esteem had been tied up in what I did and how I looked, not to mention how much I produced!

"I've been writing in my journal about you. These are my private collections of thoughts. I've been learning a lot lately. Maybe you could say I'm taking a course in life management. Anyway, you and Ramon are in my book.

"I have a job, but I'm not working right now. You could say I'm taking a little vacation. Anyway, I just enjoy coming here. I hope it's OK."

Her eyes were fixed on the white notebook.

"I'd like to read it. No one has ever written anything about me. What did you say?"

"Oh, I said that I noticed you and felt happy when we learned each other's name the other day. I said I wanted to learn from you."

"Learn from me? I didn't even finish high school. What can you learn from me?"

"Well, Sarah, we will simply have to spend time together to know that," I assured her.

She smiled. "I get breaks. I could take them in the morning with you. Maybe we could talk then."

"Sarah! Would you? I would love that. Tomorrow?"

"Tomorrow!"

Early the following morning I joined the ranks of the hungry working force. Rather than choosing the shorter line, I chose Sarah's. She was not the fastest person on the cash register, but I was not exactly in a hurry.

If self-worth was tied to having something significant to do, and somewhere you perceive as important to go, well, I certainly was not a candidate.

Sarah spotted me. She looked different. Her hair was clean and combed neatly with an ornament holding it in place. Her uniform was ironed and she had on makeup, even though it was a little uneven.

I leaned over the counter and whispered. "Do you have a date today? You look wonderful!"

She laughed. "Yea, you! No, Marsha. You are the one that I think looks terrific. I have a break at 7:30. Is that OK?"

"You bet. I'll be waiting."

I handed her the two quarters for the coffee.

"No, it's on me today," she insisted.

I smiled and accepted Sarah's simple gift of a cup of coffee. Thoughts of a coffee cup ministry began to emerge in my imagination and create strong feelings of worth and esteem. As I walked to my table to spread out my notebook and books, I thought, "What is beauty, anyway? Is it something we project? Is it physical?" I did know that Sarah was becoming more beautiful to me every day.

The first visit seemed awkward for both Sarah and me. I simply asked questions. She talked freely, yet never looked directly into my eyes.

Sarah was from a poor family. She was young, unmarried, and the mother of a 15-month-old baby girl. The more she talked, the more I realized we had absolutely nothing in common. Somehow, though, we seemed to have the ability to celebrate the differences in our lives.

Sarah had not completed high school. She was living with her mother but hoped soon to buy a mobile home. This purchase would be the first major expenditure in her life. Sarah had spent her entire life in Irving, Texas—a bedroom community of Dallas. She had never traveled out of a 30-mile radius of the Dallas/Irving area.

How did my life-style compare to Sarah's? I had traveled in nearly every state and many foreign countries. I had three college degrees and was planning for a fourth. She was a mother. I was not. I was from a Christian background. She knew nothing about Jesus. I was in my 30s. She was 17. Our body sizes were different. Our hobbies lacked any commonality. She enjoyed spending free time watching TV. I enjoyed reading, writing, and creating. Oh, but what difference did it make? None! Together we learned to celebrate our differences.

What we had in common was far more than age, hobbies, and life-style. Our bond came from one thing. We were both hungry for acceptance and self-worth. Sarah accepted me and treated me as important; I accepted and respected her. We were, as the saying goes, simply one beggar telling another beggar where we could both find bread.

My visits with Sarah became almost daily. Weeks, months, soon almost a year passed. Ramon and the others began to dominate my thoughts. My relationships with them became significant. The Golden Arches became a sanctuary from a potential storm that was mandating my leave of absence. My daily habits soon included the visit to the fast-food restaurant. I was addicted to the love, acceptance, and the ability to see beyond myself. I saw needs far different than my own. My self-centered life began to change and expand in its focus. I began to identify a field that was unreaped. This field responded to what I had to give.

Even though I was weak physically, I felt strong when I was with Sarah and Ramon. I was a strength to these new friends who earlier I would have never noticed. I began to see a field of ministry outside my own window.

"How could God use me?" I thought often. I was tired. I was sick. I was spent. How could God use someone like me in Sarah's and Ramon's lives? Then I remembered. The power of ministry did not come within my strength. He was the Source of power. The same power used to feed the thousands with a loaf of bread could be used by Him through me to feed Sarah and Ramon.

During these months I learned some of the greatest lessons of my life. My new friends taught me about real love, acceptance, and humility.

Because of Sarah and Ramon I learned I did not have to work in a Christian profession to have a personal ministry. My ministry and own self-esteem should not be so tied to a place or job that when I was not there I was not effective. It was during the time of furlough that I inducted myself into a small fraternity of those persons called "ragpickers."

I got the ragpicking idea from Og Mandino's book *The Greatest Miracle in the World*. Mandino describes an old man whose purpose in life was simply to be a ragpicker. For those of us who had escaped the period of the Great Depression, a definition of ragpicker was in order. According to Mandino, a ragpicker made it his or her occupation to search for wasted materials discarded by others.

In a brief interview with this junk man Mandino questioned why anyone would become a ragpicker by choice. Mandino insisted these are trying days but not days of depression. The elderly gentleman suggested quietly that he was not that kind of ragpicker. What he sought was much more valuable than cans or paper. He was in search for waste of the human kind, people who had been rejected by others, people whose potential was stymied by their loss of self-esteem and motivation for a better life. When he found them he tried to give them a renewed desire to live. He considered that the greatest miracle in the world.[1]

Suddenly, I began to realize that being a ragpicker of persons was my kind of business.

I decided that my new "business" must go one step further; however, I was convinced that I must not only accept those who were rejected by others but also be willing to be accepted. I needed to allow others the joy of being used to extend God's good to me. By denying anyone the opportunity to give to me, I denied God's love to be channeled through them. When we are channels for God's love to flow self-esteem really starts. Maybe self-esteem should really be called God-esteem. If so, I could not be selective about who could minister to me. I would also not be selective about those with whom I ministered. The who made no difference. The results could make all the difference in the world.

I soon learned that what I received from others must be anointed with love, respect, and willingness on my part to learn from them. Therefore, everyone, everything, and anytime could become my teacher. It was then that I began to learn something awesome about myself. I realized that a dignity denied deepened my humility. By being willing to learn from those whom I had always classified as "lower" than myself—those who had been rejected by others for any reason—physical, emotional, social, and even spiritual—I learned something marvelous about myself and my Father.

Sarah taught me about a life I had never known. I taught Sarah about a life she had never known. Together we gave each other a reason to live and to fight to become all God wanted us to become. The love and compassion that we shared were contagious. Soon the little fraternity of ragpickers spread to Ramon, Teri, and even Barb, the supervisor. They became my reason for getting up in the morning and for going to bed early.

I began to pray for an opportunity to share with Sarah my faith in Jesus Christ. The opportunity came during one of our regular coffee-break visits several months later. After explaining where the joy came from in my life and how she too could have it, I concluded by sharing that I never wanted to forget this "winter" of my life. It was during these days of what I had earlier in my life defined as a period of lack of productivity and esteem that I learned to live and recognize God's esteem.[2]

Recognize Your Esteem in Jesus Christ

Running deep within each of us is a plea for acceptance. We call this plea self-esteem. We crave acceptance, but we often feel rejection.

Whether or not rejection is real is of no significance to the one feeling rejected. The degree to which we feel rejected varies, and we usually deal with it by using various escapes.

Why do we feel such rejection inside? Are we not more than bodies? According to Genesis, we are unlike any other of God's creations. We were "created in His own image" (Gen. 1:27 NIV).

Real acceptance and esteem come when the body and soul learn to accept each other. This acceptance is internal and has eternal implications.

Our limitations diminish and our own magnificence increases as we begin to accept ourselves completely. Such acceptance is not self-consciousness. Rather, it is self-esteem rooted in God-esteem.

As we identify Whose we are and our kingdom heritage, our position in life is elevated naturally. After all, our Father created us and the universe. He also created all of the "Sarahs" in the world. To reject the Sarahs is to reject the Creator. To accept the Sarahs is to demonstrate an enormous level of God-esteem. When I accept others, I no longer have a need to judge, justify, or to set the record straight when it comes to relationships.

Such identity frees me to see through the eyes of humility— eyes that do not compare, eyes that simply focus on caring. There is no need to think about the way it used to be or could be—only the way it is. I can celebrate!

Because we share the same Creator, no one is below anyone else. Likewise, no person is above another. We are all created by the Creator in His own image. Therefore, to put others down is only putting ourselves down. It is a personal demotion. It is a symptom of our own lack of God-esteem. It says we have refused to recognize that the same Creator created all persons—you, them, and us.

To be willing to learn from others, regardless of the world's view of their position in life, may well be the highest example of security, not to mention learning.

To be a ragpicker of the human kind emulates the life-style of Jesus Christ. He suffered rejection, yet He loved and accepted others in far greater proportion than His rejection. If He can accept those who falsely accused Him, those who beat Him, those who murdered Him, can I not choose to accept all persons—including myself? It is then, and only then, that I am exalted in humility—God-esteem.

What is self-esteem? What is God-esteem? Are they the same thing? Or does one build upon the other? What difference does it make anyway, especially when it comes to a witness?

The answer to these questions could make an important difference not only in our lives, but in the eternal life of someone else. Self-esteem as it relates to the personal witness and to others is often overlooked but is crucial to the winner.

I am convinced what we perceive about ourselves on the inside is projected on the outside. How we feel about ourselves also reflects how we feel about God. It is a gauge by which we can measure our self-love rooted in God's love for us. If we have weak self-images, I believe chances are good that we will have ineffective witness. One's witness might even be in proportion to the strength of one's esteem.

Persons who have an effective witness have also usually developed strong feelings of self-worth and confidence. They have made it a habit to like themselves.

How do we develop good self-esteem? Positive feelings about ourselves must be rooted deeply in Whose we are. This feeling is the beginning of God-esteem.

A solid concept cannot be bought. Self-help books on how to increase self-esteem fill bookstores. These books cannot produce self-esteem. However, when we identify ourselves with being God's own unique creation, we identify ourselves with Him. We recognize our magnificence in Him, not our own magnificence. All that we are and potentially can be result from recognition of God being the Source of esteem.

Self-esteem is the result of fully recognizing God within.

Therefore, let us take a closer look at God-esteem, and then see how the development of this esteem can destroy feelings of lack and limitation that can be Satan's best source in dampening our witness.

God-esteem

Read Genesis 1. Are these words not incredible? We have been made in His own image. Look at yourself. You are fantastic for many reasons.

First, you are *you*. Of all the people God has ever invented, He created only one you. He has given you the gift of *you*.

Put out your hands. Look at them. They are magnificent. They are rare. They are marvelous. Feel your eyes. Within those eyes are millions of receptors with which to see the snow as it falls, to see the seasons as they change, and to see a child as he or she grows.

You have two ears with which to hear the rolling of the thunder, the wind as it sweeps through the trees, and the words, "I love you!"

Say something. That is correct; I am asking you to speak aloud. Listen to your voice. Your voice can encourage those who are depressed. It can affirm those who feel abused. How are you using your voice?

Consider your body. It may be a little out of shape, but regardless, take inventory. He has given us bodies that can move, that can reach out and love, and give to others God-esteem.

There is more still. Your body has within it over 600 muscles, 200 bones, 700 miles of nerves so synchronized by God that it is truly a walking miracle.

Since the beginning of time, God has never made anything like you. There is only one you!

You are a snowflake. You are rare. You are *you*.

"Wake up. O, sleeper, rise from the dead" (Eph. 5:14 NIV). It is only when we wake up that we can truly come to know who we are. As we awaken to the magnificence of being created in His image, we are in a position to truly recognize our esteem, God-esteem.

God-esteem means striving not to walk as your brother, or talk as your leader. It means never being anything but yourself—the self God created you to be. Show your rarity to the world. Celebrate your difference.

Ah, it sounds so wonderful and easy, you may think. But how do we start changing our mental, emotional, and spiritual picture of ourselves?

The Scriptures give us clear directions. "Do not conform to the patterns of the world, but be transformed by the renewing of your mind" (Rom. 12:2). "I have searched you. I know you. I know when you sit, when you lie down, when you stand. I know your thoughts, your ever spoken words. I have laid my hand on you. . . . There is none other like you. I have made you. And you are wonderfully made" (Psalm 139:1-5,14).

Christ has no body except me. He has no hands, except my own, with which to give Himself away, no feet to take His message to the lost except my own. God-esteem is the foundation for self-esteem. Without it, His message may never be told. He has nobody but you and me.

Once our God-esteem is established firmly, self-esteem takes care of itself. We no longer have to search outside ourselves for self-esteem for it is within.

The result of God-esteem is self-esteem. Take a closer look at self-esteem.

Self-esteem

Self-esteem may be one of the most important keys needed for developing an attitude that can make a difference in the world. It is not to be confused with self-centeredness, as we will see later. Instead, it may be the opposite.

Do a self-esteem check. Ask yourself these questions.

• Do I really like myself?
• If I could be anyone in the world, would it be me?
• Do I see myself as made in God's image?
• Do I recognize my strengths and abilities that make me special and different than anyone else?

If you can answer yes to these questions, you are on your way toward being a LIVINGtouch witness.

Where did low self-esteem come from? Are we born with it? Certainly not. Low self-esteem is a result of layers and layers of messages passed down from significant others. Many times such messages bear absolutely no truth. Even as children we were bombarded with constant reminders of lack and limitation.

"Don't interrupt; children should be seen and not heard!" "Big boys don't cry." "Don't you get angry with me; I'll give you something to cry about."[3] After a while even children get the message that they lack self-worth.

I shall never forget one of my elementary school teachers. This well-meaning teacher was trying to teach hygiene, but in her attempt she humiliated one student. She simply called two students forward. She used one to demonstrate how we should keep our nails and hair clean. The other student was the example of the child with dirty fingernails and hair. Even though I was only nine years old, I felt sorry for this student who was being picked on. I decided also I did not want to play with kids with dirty fingernails and hair. Another message was communicated to me. If I am to be liked, I must have perfect hair and nails. Today, my friends will testify that my nails are never without polish and my hair must be perfect. A college roommate once said, "Marsha, I really think you judge the worth and productivity of your day depending upon how perfect your hair turns out!"

Poor self-esteem does not stop with childhood. The constant negative bombardment from the media takes its toll. Think of the many commercials that tell us what we lack. However, the childhood experience seems to have the biggest influence. Low achievers in life encourage inferior feelings with their imaginations. These inferior feelings grow ever stronger and more harmful throughout the years. In dealing with these feelings we waver between a healthy sense of humility and a damaging sense of worthlessness. Though adults, we still have those childhood feelings. Persons with low self-esteem are always listening and accepting negative comments as real.

How do we recognize persons with low self-esteem?

We can start by listening. The person with low self-esteem is usually the one yelling loudest for attention and service. What they may really be saying is: "Help, look at me!" They are often braggarts and speak negatively about persons in authority. They protest loudly and are quick to judge others and make "put-down" statements. But underneath this exterior, is a soft, inner person wanting to be dependent.

Second, watch for symptoms of low self-esteem. Persons lacking self-esteem are usually not close to anyone else simply because they lack trust, experience self-doubt, and are jealous. Making demands in relationships and becoming offended easily are true symptoms of low self-esteem.

Dress and personal grooming can also be a clue. But sloppy dress is not the only clue. Excessive self-adoration is often an attempt to buy the fountain of youth and superficial esteem. Outward appearance is usually a reflection of inner feelings.

I recently had an interesting experience regarding outward appearance. Because of a small injury on my left earlobe, I had minor plastic surgery to correct the problem. I was amazed at the number of women getting plastic surgery. The waiting room was filled with beautiful women with one thing in common. Each wanted to look better.

When Dr. Maxwell Maltz, plastic surgeon and author, began studying people who came to him for cosmetic surgery, he discovered the importance of the self-image. He reported his amazement about people who showed dramatic and sudden changes in character and personality when a facial defect was corrected. Yet Dr. Maltz and other plastic surgeons also learned from case after case that no matter how drastic the change in appearance, certain patients insist that they looked the same as before. Their feelings of low self-esteem were so deeply ingrained they could not accept their new image.

Our generation has been called the plastic generation. Not only is this true because of the epidemic to have plastic surgery to lift our faces and put tucks in appropriate places or to add or take away pounds. We are plastic as we consider our lack of authenticity and the ease with which we obtain things. Credit cards are proof of our plastic generation. Self-esteem goes far deeper than plastic cards, skin, or possessions.

Third, feel the emotions of a self-hating person. Have you ever been with someone who you felt was overwhelmed with fear? The fear of failure, fear of success, fear of lack and limitation—the list of fears is endless. Low esteem can be observed in fearful persons, while those with too high an esteem struggle with pride.

Can low esteem self-images be changed? Of course they can! The Scripture are clear. "I can do all things through Him who strengthens me" (Phil. 4:13 NIV). I believe we can change the way we feel about ourselves. I cannot underestimate the importance of changing toward a God-esteem concept. A LIVINGtouch witness is so much more effective when the person sharing Christ has a strong concept of herself as a result of recognizing God within. After all, who is attracted to a personality that is so inconsistent with what the Bible says about who we should be in Christ? (See Gal. 5:22.)

Celebrate the Magnetic Witness Through God-esteem

Can we change our self-esteem and move toward being a magnetic and fruitful witness? If so, how?

The answer, of course, is yes! First, we must tell ourselves the truth about ourselves. As we confess these feelings in prayer, the Father supplies the wisdom and guidance we need.

Such guidance includes:

• Not concentrating on past failures.

• Always trying to look your best. After all, you are representing the Father.

• Accepting who you are and who you are not at the moment. This means avoiding comparisons with others. (I read a bumper sticker that reinforced this truth: God's not through with me yet!)

• Accepting responsibility for mistakes and successes. Remember, it is OK to say thank you when given a compliment.

• Talking to yourself. Strange? What we say to ourselves is often more important than what others say to us. Listen to yourself. Do you quietly or even mentally say, "You dummy, you can't do anything right today!" Instead, could you not replace such negative self-talk with words such as these: "I made a mistake, but I will do better next time."

• Evaluating your attitude. Attitude can work for or against you. Remember, our negative attitude about ourselves and others may be based on false information stored as real.

• Taking inventory of your blessings.

• Setting your own internal standards based on quality time spent with the Father.

• Volunteering your own name first when relating to another person. As you pay value to your own name, you are paying value to the other person as well.

• Using their name when speaking to others. Remember, many people wear name tags. Use names.

• Remembering to smile and practicing saying thank you.

• Looking people straight in the eye when involved in conversation. This action communicates not only your esteem, but the importance and self-worth of the other person as well.

• Planning a personal development strategy. What is something you want to accomplish, learn, or do? Start doing something with your plan or strategy NOW! Begin immediately.

• Making Mark 12:31 your daily motto. Put this verse on your mirror or desk: "You must love others as much as yourself." Go. Practice loving yourself.

By now I hope you are convinced of the importance of esteem. But perhaps you are still wondering what God-esteem and self-esteem have to do with making a magnetic and winning witness. I like William Clemmons's explanation of the importance of a strong inner concept. He says that the biblical understanding of the need for a healthy sense of self-esteem comes from the story of the lawyer who questioned Jesus about which was the greatest commandment.

Jesus replied in part, "You shall love your neighbor as yourself" (Mark 12:31 RSV). Self-love is the starting point of loving others. When you lower your own level of self-hate and scorn, you decrease your dislike of other people. Moreover, our love for others increases our ability to love God. First John 4:20 (TEV) points this out: "If someone says he loves God, but hates his brother, he is a liar. For he cannot love God, whom he has not seen, if he does not love his brother, whom he has seen."[4]

God does not love us because we are of value. Love based on value alone may be considered a humanistic approach to self-love that flows so freely in many popular psychological aspects toward self-fulfillment and gratification. But God loves us because *He* is valuable. Acceptance and love was and is His very nature. It is God Who made us. Our esteem is reinforced when we are constantly mindful of His value. "The Lord formed me in the beginning, before he created anything else. From ages past, I am. I existed before the earth began."

Why, then, is it so hard to love ourselves? Why do we have the idea that self-love is wrong? If self-love is wrong, there would be no need to love our neighbors as ourselves. Paul explained this. Even if you dislike yourself, you probably don't willingly go hungry. You clothe yourself as best you can. You make sure you have a place to live if at all possible.

The question remains: Is this the kind of love we are sharing with our neighbors and our neighbor's neighbors? Do we see that they are fed, clothed, and housed? What is an example of loving others as ourselves and a strong God-esteem? It may be as simple as active involvement in meeting the needs of others.

Finally, be mindful that we are not the King, but are to be responsible ambassadors of the King. As ambassadors we have a message of His love and acceptance to share with the world.

THE CHALLENGE TO TOUCH

How can your effectiveness in being a LIVINGtouch witness be strengthened? Perhaps a stronger self-esteem and God-esteem is the answer. Reread Genesis 1 and Psalm 139:14. In the space below, write answers to these questions:

1. Who are you? Examine your current strengths and weaknesses.

2. Do a self-esteem check by rating the following. (Circle 5 for yes, 3 for sometimes, 1 for rarely.)
   • Do I really like myself? 5   3   1
   • I would rather be me than anyone else in the world. 5   3   1
   • I see myself made in God's image. 5   3   1
   • I recognize my strengths and abilities that make me special, unique, and different. 5   3   1

3. What will you do today to strengthen your esteem? Look over the list on pages 50-51.

4. What plans will you make for further development of a loving self-concept?

5. Identify someone who exhibits a low self-esteem. What actions will you take to help that person feel better about herself or himself?

6. How will you make this statement true in your life: An effective, magnetic, winning witness may well start as I recognize and accept my esteem in Jesus Christ.

[1]Og Mandino, *The Greatest Miracle in the World* (New York: Bantam Books, 1979), 16.

[2]Marsha Spradlin, *Transformed One Winter* (Nashville: Broadman Press, 1989).

[3]Denis Waitley, *The Winner's Edge* (New York: Berkley Publishing, 1983), 65.

[4]William P. Clemmons, *Discovering the Depths*, rev. ed. (Nashville: Broadman Press, 1987), 19-20.

5
Giving Graciously Your Gifts

*"For it is by grace you have been saved, through faith—and this
not from yourselves, it is the gift of God—not by works, so that
no one can boast"* (Eph. 2:8-9 NIV).

THE TOUCH: AN ENCOUNTER WITH WENDY AND SUSAN

No encounter is merely coincidental. I am convinced of this
after meeting Wendy and Susan. All encounters teach us
something of ourselves, our strengths, as well as our weaknesses, if we are willing to learn from them.

I was eager to get home after a two-day consulting meeting
with other Christian leaders. It was Saturday night. According
to the flight schedule, it would be the better part of wisdom,
financially, if I spent the night in Memphis rather than returning on a peak hour flight that night. Since I was going
to have to stay anyway, my work associates made my layover
a happy experience for me by taking me to dinner at the
Memphis Peabody Hotel.

It was a delightful evening. To top it off, my friends decided
that I could not leave Memphis without a Peabody Hotel
sweatshirt. They gathered their dollar bills while they convinced me to pick out a sweatshirt. I selected a pink one with
little white ducks. It was adorable. By now, I was glad I had
stayed the extra evening. It was nearly midnight when I got
to my hotel room, too late to try on my new shirt.

Since the plane was scheduled to leave about noon, I decided to spend the morning catching up on correspondence while enjoying a late breakfast. I put on my jeans, tennis shoes, and the new Peabody Hotel sweatshirt instead of my usual two-piece suit and heels. It was then that I realized that the size small indicated in the sweatshirt was indeed small. By mistake, I had gotten a child's small instead of an adult small.

While I am not considered a large person by anyone's estimation, the child's small sweatshirt would fit only over one arm. I was frustrated, angry, and thinking quickly of ways to exchange the shirt before leaving town at noon. I called the hotel gift shop. It did not open until noon. By that time, I would be well on my way to Birmingham.

I resolved finally that I would have to mail the shirt back. Why this decision was so upsetting I am not sure.

I managed to pull something together to wear to breakfast, gathered my briefcase, and rushed quickly to the elevator. It seemed to stop on every floor. I assumed that someone had pushed every button and then gotten off. I was fuming.

At about the 11th floor, I had to stop myself and dialogue quickly with the Father. "What is going on, Father?" I confessed. "Forgive me for letting outside circumstances control my thoughts, attitudes, and ability to praise You. This is the day You have made. Help me to rejoice in it. If You can use any of my frustrations for Your advantage, I trust You will do so. Turn this day around fast."

It was a fast turnaround. The elevator door opened on the 9th floor. This time two people joined me.

The woman, slightly older than myself, looked worn, tired, upset, and in grief. Her eyes were bloodshot and her hair rather disarrayed. She was pushing a wheelchair. In the chair was a young girl, maybe 12 years old. She was obviously very ill. She hardly looked up. The little girl was frail, weak, and sad. She had on a pink sweatshirt.

Elevators are the perfect place to stare at the ceiling. It seems we have been taught to stare at the elevator numbers to avoid making eye contact with other persons in the elevator. While I wanted to disappear, to escape the uncomfortable setting, I could not. To make matters worse, the three of us could not avoid seeing each other clearly. The elevator was covered in mirrors, wall to wall, ceiling to floor. So I reached deep inside for something appropriate to say.

"I have a pink sweatshirt almost like yours, except mine doesn't fit. Yours looks wonderful. I only wish I could say the same about mine."

The little girl did not notice that I was talking to her, but her mother picked up on the cue.

By this time the elevator had stopped on the ground level. The restaurant was just around the corner. As I said good-bye and started walking toward the restaurant, I noticed that they were also headed for breakfast.

The hostess greeted us as a group.

"Three for breakfast?" she said.

"No, we aren't together. I'm separate. Go ahead and seat them first. I am in no hurry."

"Oh, yes, we are together," the mother insisted quickly. Looking at me for approval she continued, "Please, a table for three."

"Sure, I would be glad to join you for breakfast. Thank you for inviting me."

Inside I thought, "Well, forget catching up on correspondence."

Special arrangements were made to accommodate the wheelchair. The dining room was filled to capacity. I noticed those seated nearby observing our special accommodation and looking intensely at the little girl. I wanted suddenly to protect her from their stares.

Just as we were seated, with menus in hand, Susan, the mother, asked to be excused. "I'll be right back. I have to make some phone calls." She was gone.

I glanced at the frail little girl. "I'm Marsha. What's your name?"

"Wendy."

"Well, Wendy, I'm hungry. What looks good to you?"

"Nothing."

"Let's see. What about chocolate milk? Do you like toast and maybe an egg?"

"I guess."

The waitress came, and I ordered. In moments breakfast was arranged beautifully on our table. Wendy's mother was not back. I decided we should go ahead with our meal without her.

"Do you think your mom would mind? I don't want that toast to get cold."

"It's OK. She's probably talking to my daddy."

Wendy and I started eating. Wendy was slow and very awkward. After only a bite or two, she suddenly stopped eating. She froze. I could tell something was wrong. I was frightened. As I reached for her, she threw up everything, everywhere. I learned instantly that one does not have to be a mother to have maternal instincts. I reached for the nearest cloth napkin, stuck it in the glass of ice water, and wrapped it around her neck. The waitresses observed the trauma, and acted like nurses rather than waitresses. One quickly removed everything from the table, tablecloth included, while the others brought cold towels and a blanket.

"I feel better now," Wendy said.

It was then that I noticed that we were the center of attention for everyone. Wendy did look better, but her pretty pink sweatshirt was no longer pretty pink.

I looked at the waitress. "We have to get her cleaned up," I said.

I reached into my pocket for my room key as one waitress stood nearby. "Can you go to my room and look on the bed? There is a pink Peabody Hotel sweatshirt. Get it. I'll meet you in the ladies room just outside the restaurant. If we're lucky we can have this little angel fixed up before her mother gets back."

The waitress rushed off. I unlocked the wheelchair and proceeded with my assignment. In moments the waitress returned with the sweatshirt. Perfect timing, not to mention a perfect fit.

"It looks beautiful on you, Wendy!"

I reached into my purse for a brush. We repaired her tangled hair before returning to the restaurant.

When we wheeled back to the table, the waitresses had not only reset the table, but had reordered for us. Fresh toast, chocolate milk, coffee, and my muffins were waiting. Wendy ate. I sipped my coffee and looked at each waitress with an expression of relief and thanks!

Susan returned. After ordering breakfast she noticed

Wendy was eating. Then she noticed the sweatshirt.

"Honey, where did you get that sweatshirt?"

As Wendy explained the story to her mom, I observed the many onlookers listening. I wondered what was going through their minds.

"Marsha, we can't take the shirt. I feel awful about leaving you. How can I thank you for what you did for me this morning?"

"Susan, how can I thank you? I think I have fallen in love with your daughter. If you had not left, well, that might not have happened. Please let her keep the shirt. She's my new friend. So are you. I hate to eat and rush, but I have to pack. My plane leaves in an hour."

I reached into my briefcase and scratched out a note.

Susan:
I don't know the circumstances here but I am sure you are hurting. It is obvious that Wendy is very ill. I want to pray for you. Here is a self-addressed, stamped envelope. Will you write and tell me how she is doing? Will you tell me how I can help you? I don't think it is a coincidence that we met. I pledge my prayer support. I do love your daughter! I love you too.
Marsha Spradlin

I handed the note to Susan as I left. She squeezed my hand and wiped a tear. I did the same. I then wrapped my arms around Wendy. Meanwhile, Susan jotted her address on the paper napkin.

"I gave your mom my address. Will you write me?"

"Sure I will! I have a teacher that comes to my house every week. She can help me."

I took the ticket to the counter to pay. I thanked the waitresses for their help.

"You didn't even know that lady?" one waitress asked.

"No, actually, we met in the elevator!"

"Why were you so nice, and why did you give her that shirt?"

"Why were you so nice?" I insisted. "I guess God just planted us together this morning to be a team. You were all terrific. I plan to write your supervisor and tell her so."

It had been two or three weeks since the episode in Memphis. I had wondered often about them. My concern for them was relieved only as I prayed for my new friends. Meanwhile, I realized that the Saint Jude's Hospital for children was within blocks of the hotel where we were staying. I began to put pieces of the puzzle together. Obviously, Wendy was in Memphis for outpatient treatment. I was right.

As I flipped through my mail after a long day at the office, I noticed a letter with unfamiliar writing. The return address was Gulfport, Mississippi.

"Who do I know in Gulfport?" I wondered. I dropped everything and ripped open the letter.

April 4, 1986

Dear Marsha:

I really believe God works in our lives and through us. I know He is at work through you, because I felt it in your voice and actions. There was a reason for us both being at the hotel that Sunday morning, and it has made a difference in our lives. Wendy enjoys wearing her Peabody shirt, and we like our new children's missions magazines that you are sending.

Wendy will be at Saint Jude's Hospital April 8-12 again for chemotherapy. She has a brain tumor. We thought it was all over last summer when the tumor was removed. Then, the day before I met you, I learned that it had returned, and that she would eventually die. She has a year, if we are lucky. Well, the news was devastating. That is why I had to go. I had to talk to my husband, Jerry.

I think of you often.

We love you,
Susan and Wendy

From that moment Wendy became my personal prayer project. Susan became a person easily identified as one starving for love and strength. We began to correspond on a regular basis. I continued to send Wendy a children's missions magazine. Susan and I exchanged Bible verses, clippings from cards, articles, etc., that had messages of hope. I knew I could not be with her physically, but I could be with her through the Father's love.

I had recognized a year or two earlier that one of my spiritual gifts was encouragement. I was determined to use that gift in Wendy and Susan's lives. Meanwhile, I realized I needed to know if Susan was aware of the Source of strength that could be hers through the Father. I learned through our correspondence that Susan was a Christian. That assurance was comforting. I was discomforted, however, in learning, or relearning, that Christians are not exempt from pain, suffering, and the need to be the recipients of ministry. I realized as I shared this experience with Susan, Wendy, and Jerry, that there were times when it was difficult to even get a glimpse of God's goodness. I could stretch to my tiptoes searching for faith, hoping to catch a vision of the hidden mysteries behind pain and suffering. I had to simply trust that He knew more about pain and suffering than all of us. Together, Susan and I realized that during those moments of stretching the Father always directs us back to the beginning, His love. We clung to that love.

December 1986

Dearest Marsha:
    Our Wendy is in a semicoma and is not expected to live very long. She cannot talk or communicate in any way. We don't think she can see. She was released from chemo on October 28 because the tumor was growing in spite of the treatment. We would like to thank you for your prayers and concern since we met.
        We love you!
        Wendy, Susan, and Jerry

These were helpless times for me. I could imagine the helpless feeling that Susan must have been experiencing as she watched Wendy grow weaker. I wanted to catch the first plane to Gulfport and simply embrace Susan. Yet I knew the embrace was already there. I had to claim victory in spite of my interpretation of what was good. I could pray, I could encourage, and I did have a pen and notepad. The correspondence was consistent. The prayers were constant.

Weeks passed. I heard nothing. I tried to call, but no one answered the phone. I received a letter from Susan on February 10, 1987. Instead of tearing through the envelope to learn of Wendy's progress, I simply placed it in my purse. I knew I did not want to know what was written in the letter. I carried the letter around inside my purse for four days. Finally, I felt embraced with God's peace. I opened the letter.

February 6, 1987

Dearest Marsha:
    Wendy is with God now. She died January 5, 1987, at 1:00 A.M.

She died at home with her family, doctor, nurse, and our pastor at her side. I am enclosing a picture and the news article.

Thank you for all your help and prayers. We prayed for a miracle and now Wendy has the best miracle of all.

God bless you,
Susan and Jerry

Yes, Wendy was now experiencing the best miracle of all. Because of God's infinite love for us, Wendy was now with Him. That is the greatest miracle of all. I wept. I grieved for days. Finally, I wrote:

My dear friend Susan:

Did you know I was in love with your daughter? She, and you, touched my life. I shall never be the same. Because of Wendy's courage, your faith, and our Father's love, I am now more committed than ever before to live a life that can make a difference in the world.

Not every "Wendy" has a Christian mother. Not everyone is a Christian. I have one life to live. I want it to count. I want my life to count for Wendy too. Wendy has given me the courage to make it count.

I will use my pain as energy to tell the world about the greatest miracle of all!

I love you,
Marsha

Allowing God to Use Our Gifts

My encounter with Wendy and Susan was not a bright encounter. Instead, it was a dark and painful experience. It was an experience that caused me to examine how God could possibly use me to minister and share His strength. My own inadequacy was frustrating at times. Of all the people in the world, why did God choose me to have breakfast with Wendy and Susan that Sunday morning in February 1986? I shall never know the answer to that question. But, reflections of that encounter have taught me several things. My inadequacy does not count. My availability to be used by God does.

Have you ever thought about the people Jesus selected to become His disciples? There was not one in the entire bunch who qualified to be a disciple. If we did a detailed, theological study, we would learn that these men were common, and maybe even a little below average according to the standards of the time. They were not wealthy, not necessarily intelligent, not witty or charming. Yet, they were chosen. We do not choose God; He chooses us! Consider these Scripture verses:

"But I choose you to go and bear fruit" (John 15:16).
"He chose us in Him before the creation" (Eph. 1:4).
"From the beginning God chose you" (2 Thess. 2:13).
"For many are invited, but few are chosen" (Isa. 41:8).
"But I have chosen you out of the world" (John 15:19).
"But you are a chosen people" (1 Peter 2:9).

How could God use me? He has an investment in me. He had already chosen me. When you were small, did you ever play games in which you were chosen? Do you remember how you felt when you were picked? Do you remember the feelings of rejection when you were not picked? Not being the athletic type, I was not always first to be picked, but when I was, I was so excited that I was determined to do the best I could to prove worthy of being picked first.

Regardless of how much I do, I cannot prove worthy of being picked by God. But I can demonstrate my appreciation by being one who polishes her potential. I can communicate my appreciation for being picked by developing my many facets and dimensions. This action says, "I love you, Father. Thank you for picking me to be your ambassador." What good is it to polish my ability and then to keep it to myself?

We cannot love God with all our hearts and then keep our hearts to ourselves. We must use what God has given us to serve others.

What He has given each of us is not the same. It is true that God offers salvation, love, and the fruit of the spirit to each believer. But abilities and spiritual gifts are custom designed according to what the Father needs to be accomplished in His world. We are snowflakes, each created in His image for specific duties, tasks, and responsibilities.

Charles Schulz's famous Peanuts cartoon illustrates this point in a clever, yet realistic way in the feature "Good Ol' Charlie Brown."

Let me fill you in on the setting. Snoopy has determined

to get into shape physically. He obviously is intending to polish his potential. On his first trip out, he is jogging alone and thinking hard—some call it self-talk—to redirect his attention from the pain that often comes in attempting to get into shape. Each part of his little dog body speaks in an attempt to convince Snoopy of its superiority.

The nose, the ear, the heart, the foot, all take turns expounding on why they are important and should receive top consideration. Yet, by the end of the run, each part of the body has realized not only its own contributions, but its dependency on the rest of the body.

I am sure you will agree that we belong to the same body, and that we all have roles and responsibilities. If each of us takes our responsibilities seriously and polishes our own potential to become all that God has intended for us to become, we can make a profound difference in the world. But it will take all of us. We are each an important part of a winning body.

As part of that body, we can first polish our potential by:

Recognizing Our Spiritual Gifts

One of the precious truths concerning the ministry of the Holy Spirit is that He has blessed each of us with particular abilities and strengths. The Bible refers to these strengths as spiritual gifts. No Christian is exempt. We all have at least one spiritual gift. Every Christian is given special abilities to use in serving Christ. God holds us responsible for the way we use our gifts.

There is still another precious truth. Just as the physical body depends on the certain mixture of natural elements which compose it, the body of Christ depends upon the special blending of believers' gifts and abilities. Paintings cannot be depicted with one color, and symphonies demand more than one kind of note. Even so does spiritual creativity exist through the combination of differently gifted believers.

The Father has promised to equip us spiritually even for the smallest task. We cannot ignore His commission to be His witnesses. While we may feel weak, afraid, immobile, and impoverished at times, He has already supplied the talents, strengths, abilities, and gifts needed for the task. Such gifts will differ depending on the task. Yet the service qualifications for every Christian are the same. Each one of us has been gifted to serve—called to act.

Take a look at the meaning of gifts.

Like so many words in the English language, the words *gift* and *gifts* are used in a variety of ways. "He has a gift for that." "She is so gifted." "That was a gift from heaven."

In the spiritual arena of our lives, however, the word *gift* describes that which is given to each believer at the moment of salvation. Acts 2:38 (TEV) says, "Each one of you must turn away from his sins and be baptized in the name of Jesus Christ, so that your sins will be forgiven; and you will receive God's gift, the Holy Spirit."

Spiritual gifts make us aware of God's presence and activity in our lives and in His church. It is the work of believers, you and me, in the church to worship, witness, minister, and have fellowship. To equip us for that assignment, the Spirit of God gives *charismata*, the Greek word for spiritual gifts, so the church can function as a family doing God's will. His will can be accomplished both privately, individually, and through the corporate body, the church.

We do not choose our gifts. In her book, *Yours for the Giving: Spiritual Gifts*, Barbara Joiner makes it clear we should not even ask for particular gifts. First Corinthians 12:11 says, "But it is one and the same Spirit who does all this; as He wishes, he gives a different gift to each person."

I once heard of a small boy named Jonathan. In Sunday School, Jonathan's teacher asked him where he got his name. She was thinking of course that there was significance behind the name. Maybe they were studying the story of David and Jonathan. Jonathan's answer to the question was precise. "I was just born this way." As Christians, we, like Jonathan, are just born this way, with a gift.

I am reminded again of Snoopy when I examine 1 Corinthians 12:21. These verses are a lesson in anatomy of the human body and the church. It is clear that even though the foot, the eye, the hand, the ear, and other parts are different, they all make up one body, and each part is essential. In the church, we are all different. We each have different gifts, but all of the gifts are necessary to fulfill God's purpose.

Have you ever had a toothache, headache, or some rather

insignificant pain? If you have, you suddenly realized the importance of that part of the body that is suffering. Even though the rest of the body may be strong, one small tooth, when under stress, can literally ground the entire strong body for days. There is no insignificant part of the body. It is obvious, then, that gifts are not given for individual advancement, prestige, or for competitiveness. They are given for the glory of God and building up of the church. For this reason we are to be modest. There is no room for bragging about the gift given, and there is no reason for being jealous by comparing gifts.

Take a moment and read the following passages concerning spiritual gifts. Use the King James Version if it is available. Either circle the gifts listed or jot them down in the margin of this book.

Read Romans 12:6-13; 1 Corinthians 12:8-10, 28-30; Ephesians 4:11; and 1 Peter 4:10-11. Did you find 23 gifts? Some are duplications. Here is Barbara Joiner's list: prophecy, ministering, teaching, exhorting or encouraging, giving, ruling, mercy, love, fervency or enthusiasm, hope, prayer, hospitality, wisdom, knowledge, faith, healing, miracles, discerning of spirits, tongues, interpretation of tongues, apostleship, evangelism, pastoring.

This list is not exhaustive. I am sure other gifts could be added. Some theologians add love as a spiritual gift and some would not list prayer as a gift.

Gifts Are to Be Graciously Given

How do you know which gift is yours? I feel there are five ways to know. First, prayer. As I pray, God can reveal to me my spiritual gift or gifts. Second, through examination of the Scriptures. Third, contemplating your most basic desires and inclinations. What is it that you enjoy doing the most or are best at? Our spiritual gift is usually something we enjoy doing anyway. And fourth, we usually receive affirmation from fellow Christians who have observed that gift(s) in us.

The fifth way, however, is perhaps the most important. As we give our gift away in ministry and witnessing we are not only recognizing the gift, but we are also sharing the good and perfect Gift, Jesus Christ, with the world. A spiritual gift becomes a free gift when it is given away!

65

I believe my personal spiritual gifts include encouraging, mercy, teaching, and enthusiasm. I feel more like me when I am exercising these gifts. There is nothing I enjoy doing more than encouraging other believers and enthusiastically teaching His truths. Perhaps that is why it is so easy for me to converse with someone on a plane, or teach a seminar, or write a book.

I do not have the gift of hospitality. If you come to my home for dinner, please bring your own frozen TV dinner. I do have a microwave. While I do not have this gift, I have a good friend who does have the gift of hospitality. Beth is the perfect hostess. She enjoys cooking, planning menus, inviting guests, and she does it with such ease. When I try to pull off such an evening, I am a wreck. What a relief it was to realize that I do not have to be all things to all people at all times.

Remember, He decides the gift. We receive it graciously.

What do spiritual gifts have to do with personal witnessing? Everything!

Earlier in this book I said that it will take all of us to touch the lost for Jesus Christ. It will also take a variety of approaches. Not everyone can comfortably get into a conversation with a total stranger on an airplane. Likewise, not all of us can prepare a meal and open our homes for our new neighbors across the street. Each of these are ways to touch the lives of non-Christians. Whatever your gift, use it as a platform for sharing the gospel.

THE CHALLENGE TO TOUCH

Which gifts are yours? To find out, read these Scripture verses on spiritual gifts: Romans 12:5-13; 1 Corinthians 12:8-10, 28-30; Ephesians 4:11; 1 Peter 4:10-11.

In the space on the next page, write each gift found in the Scripture verses listed above. You may find as many as 23 gifts listed. Write them in the left column. In the right column do the five-point check described on page 65 to enable you to more fully recognize your gift(s).

• Place a circle around "Prayer" if you have prayed about this particular gift.

• Place a circle around "Examine" if you have examined the Scripture verses regarding the use of this gift.

- Place a circle around "Contemplate" if you have dwelled on your basic desires and inclinations. Do they seem to fit with this gift?
- Place a circle around "Affirmed" if you have received affirmation when you have demonstrated this gift.
- Place a circle around "Given" if you have experienced joy when you have given this gift to others.

Part 1: Identifying Your Spiritual Gifts

1. Prayer Examine Contemplate Affirmed Given
2. Prayer Examine Contemplate Affirmed Given
3. Prayer Examine Contemplate Affirmed Given
4. Prayer Examine Contemplate Affirmed Given
5. Prayer Examine Contemplate Affirmed Given
6. Prayer Examine Contemplate Affirmed Given
7. Prayer Examine Contemplate Affirmed Given
8. Prayer Examine Contemplate Affirmed Given
9. Prayer Examine Contemplate Affirmed Given
10. Prayer Examine Contemplate Affirmed Given
11. Prayer Examine Contemplate Affirmed Given
12. Prayer Examine Contemplate Affirmed Given
13. Prayer Examine Contemplate Affirmed Given
14. Prayer Examine Contemplate Affirmed Given
15. Prayer Examine Contemplate Affirmed Given
16. Prayer Examine Contemplate Affirmed Given
17. Prayer Examine Contemplate Affirmed Given
18. Prayer Examine Contemplate Affirmed Given
19. Prayer Examine Contemplate Affirmed Given
20. Prayer Examine Contemplate Affirmed Given
21. Prayer Examine Contemplate Affirmed Given
22. Prayer Examine Contemplate Affirmed Given
23. Prayer Examine Contemplate Affirmed Given

Part 2: Using Your Spiritual Gift

Review the list in part 1. Write on the next page the gift(s) which have four or five circles. Next to each gift, write the name of a nonbeliever. Now, write a sentence to describe

your plan, strategy, or approach for using your gift or gifts
to win that person to Jesus Christ.

MY GIFT(S)	NAMES OF NONBELIEVERS	MY PLANS

6
Becoming Aware of Your External World

"I tell you, take a good look at the fields; the crops are now ripe and ready to be harvested!" (John 4:35 TEV).

THE TOUCH: THE ENCOUNTER WITH ETHEL AND SARA ANN

The alarm jolted me from my warm bed at precisely 4:15 A.M. The routine was like clockwork. By 4:30 A.M. I was dressed in my warm-ups and walking out the door of my Dallas condominium toward my car. By 4:37 A.M. I entered IHOP with a stack of books and a blue notebook. The International House of Pancakes was located only one block from home. Fortunately for me, it was open 24 hours.

Each morning she seated me at the same booth by the window. She was tall, slender, in her mid-40s, and toothless. That is about all I remember about her. After all, it took all of my mental energy to be awake, much less notice anyone else. Little conversation was exchanged except, "I'll have your coffee out in one second." And she did just that. She kept the coffee cup filled.

From 4:40 until 6:30 I sat in that booth, glued to the stack of books while I consumed numerous cups of coffee. I seldom focused my eyes away from my reason for being there.

Earlier that year I made the decision to return to school. I already had a graduate degree, but realized that for me to have an effective ministry with adults, I needed more education. This realization meant sacrifice. I could not afford myself the luxury of resigning work to attend school full time. Therefore, I had to squeeze in study time. First, I had to prepare for the famous GRE (a graduate entrance examination).

The Graduate Record Examination (GRE) is required for persons seeking higher educational status. The exam is intended to weed out candidates for graduate or doctoral studies who do not exhibit the mental ability to pull it off. I was determined to pass the exam with a high enough score that graduate schools would be seeking me to be their student. I was proud of this noble ambition.

Each morning I studied. Within four months I memorized 4,000 vocabulary words, relearned geometry and algebra, polished reading comprehension skills, and learned to think analytically. Every moment not at work was spent studying. I carried vocabulary words on index cards and reviewed them while waiting in the grocery lines. I was obsessed with the challenge.

While my focus grew on my noble inner ambition, the focus on my outer world became more limited. I had set priorities. These priorities did not include people, at least for the time being.

Finally, the day came. I took the exam. Then came the hard part, waiting three months for the score. I passed!

I enrolled immediately for postgraduate studies at East Texas State University. One week after completing the first semester, I received a phone call that totally changed the direction and focus of my life. I was offered a position at the national headquarters of my organization. The job responsibility was exactly in line with my career goals. I would have the opportunity to practice doing what I had been studying. These opportunities included teaching young adults, planning adult growth strategies, and developing the programs for their spiritual development. How could I not take advantage of this new challenge?

Weeks after my first semester course at East Texas, I moved from Dallas, Texas, to Birmingham, Alabama, to assume my new job responsibilities. The job required a great deal of travel and even more mental concentration than the GRE. I decided to postpone further studies until I could get a handle on the new job and make the many adjustments.

Four months later I traveled to Fort Worth, Texas, to lead a seminar for college students interested in a missions vocation. The meeting was three days long and a new challenge. I wanted to do my best in presenting materials and making the missions challenge motivational and inspirational. I arose early to have time to add the polishing touch to my presentation.

Since I had lived in Fort Worth years earlier, I knew that there was an IHOP just down the street. I knew also that it would be open at the unusually early hour. So, I dressed quickly in a suit, starched shirt, and heels. I drove to IHOP in my rental car.

Have you ever had an experience that seemed to be a replay of a former one?

As I entered, I was greeted by a most familiar woman. She too looked at me. While we said nothing, I am certain that we both thought, "Don't I know you from somewhere?"

The tall, toothless woman seated me at a booth near the window.

"Coffee, only," I said, as I pulled out my notes.

"Somehow I knew that," was her immediate response.

I had been drinking coffee and working for several minutes when Ethel came to refill my coffee cup. She was so attentive. "I know you're very busy, but can I ask you a question?"

"Certainly, have a seat."

"Well, I feel I know you from somewhere. I was back in the kitchen telling Sara Ann, the other waitress, about you. She said, 'Ethel, just go up and ask her.' So, I'm asking. Where could we have met?"

"Ethel, it's strange that you should say that. I had those same feelings when I walked in. In fact, I've thought about it and decided maybe you simply reminded me of someone else. After all, I don't even live here. I live in Birmingham, Alabama."

"I've never even been to Alabama," Ethel replied.

Quickly I responded, "But, I used to live here, maybe ten years ago."

"No, that's not it," Ethel said. "I didn't live here then. In fact, I just moved from Dallas to Fort Worth a few months ago," she explained.

"Dallas! You lived in Dallas? That's it, Ethel."

"I was transferred from the IHOP over on Forest Lane."

"Ethel, that was me, every morning with the books and the warm-ups. You served my coffee while I studied."

"I wondered what ever happened to you," Ethel said suddenly. "You disappeared. You look so different in real clothes," she laughed.

"Can you stay for a minute? We must catch up."

Ethel did sit for over an hour as we talked. I shared what I had been doing during those months at the IHOP restaurant and what my life was like now. She shared about her son and how hard it was to hold down two jobs. She had gotten a promotion at the Fort Worth franchise. This job was helping with some of the expenses of raising a growing teenaged boy. Apparently, Ethel was separated from her husband and living with her son in a small Fort Worth apartment. Even with the promotion, I could tell she was struggling financially as well as emotionally.

"Ethel, you are delightful. How could I have missed knowing you all that time?" I asked.

Ethel stared out the window as the sun began to shimmer through the blue and purple Texas sky.

"Well, I really wanted to talk to you so many times in Dallas. In fact, we all talked about you back in the kitchen. No one could understand why anyone would get up so early and spend so much time studying. We were fascinated, to say the least. But you never looked up. In fact, I didn't think you ever saw me."

I could not respond. I knew Ethel was right. I had not seen her. My world was so focused on my self-centered inner world that I saw nothing but what I wanted to accomplish.

"Ethel, I am going to be here a couple of days. Can we make up the time?"

"Well, sure. After all, I work the night shift and don't get off till 6:00 A.M. Can you come in the morning? I want Sara Ann to meet you. Listen, I'll even buy your breakfast."

"Now, Ethel, that is an offer I can't refuse."

Early the next morning I appeared, but this time with nothing in hand, no books, no notes, just an appetite for breakfast and getting to know Ethel and Sara Ann.

The two greeted me as if I were a queen. We sat in a corner booth while each took turns cooking breakfast and visiting. During the two hours we simply "fell in love." We exchanged addresses and promised to write each other. My address was printed on a small business card, which described my job responsibility as a national consultant.

"What does this mean and why do you do it?" Sara Ann inquired.

Perfect! A chance to share my faith, my reason for being. And a second chance to focus on what really mattered—Christ in me.

As I shared my faith with Ethel and Sara Ann, they listened intently.

"Will you write us and tell us more about what you've said?"

"Of course. But, wait. I think I may have something for you—a gift."

In my purse was a small New Testament.

"I only have this one, but you can share it. I'll write, but in the meantime, will you promise to read?"

"It's a deal," Ethel said. "In fact, Sara Ann, why can't we stay an hour longer every morning and read together?"

The women agreed. Two non-Christians starting their own coffee-cup Bible study. I could hardly believe what I was experiencing. I wonder what would have happened if only I had noticed Ethel sooner?

Identifying Needs in the External World

Somehow I wanted to preserve this bright encounter with Ethel and Sara Ann. I realized something important. It is often in the commonplace of our everydayness—the routines of life—that encounters become memorable. They become so memorable they can change us for the rest of our lives.

How often do we get so caught up in our spiritual or noble affairs that we miss seeing the spiritual needs right around us? We may not see the needs because of prejudices or because they might cause us an inconvenience.

Where do we begin identifying our outer world? Most

Christians need help in identifying persons in their outer world who are nonbelievers.

Does thinking about the outer world terrify you as you consider making a LIVINGtouch difference? You may think, "How can I possibly meet all the needs out there?"

The focus of the Bible is clear. We live in one physical world, one place, and one moment at a time. Only when every believer focuses on his or her own world can the entire world be reached for Christ. The entire world! This task takes every believer, every day, every moment. We can, however, fulfill the mandate given in Matthew 28:18-20 as we go daily into our own outer worlds.

Look at the interpretation of the outer world as given in the Bible. Such investigation shows us not only our world but that we are not expected to go into our world in our own strength. Our own resources are not equal to the task. Only Jesus' strength is sufficient. With Him you always have enough. Remember, you are the salt of the world.

"But you will receive power when the Holy Spirit comes on you; and you will be my witnesses in Jerusalem, and in all Judea and Samaria, and to the ends of the earth" (Acts 1:8 NIV). Notice the progression of worlds as expressed in the verse: Jerusalem, Judea, Samaria, and the uttermost parts of the earth. This verse illustrates the nearby, where Jesus was, and the faraway, where some of us may go. Can we influence both the nearby and the far away? At the same time? Absolutely!

One of the most exciting experiences I have ever encountered in personal witnessing was through correspondence with a teenaged girl who lived far away. Though my life was a witness outside my immediate world through this experience, I still had the daily responsibility to nurture those within my own Jerusalem.

Look at Acts 1:8 again. Which world is mentioned first? Jerusalem! I believe a winning worldwide witness must begin first in our personal worlds, our own backyards, so to speak. The nearby. The Jerusalem.

Next, we can move—either physically, through correspondence, or through prayerful and financial support of missionaries—into the other three worlds. The fact remains, we have been mandated to influence all of these worlds. Our contribution to these worlds will vary, depending upon our spiritual gifts, abilities, interests, and availability.

Examine our worlds by using the following tools. In *Concentric Circles of Concern*,[1] W. Oscar Thompson, Jr., used concentric circles to identify persons within one's world who need the gospel. He began with self (1) and moved outward to Person X.

It is hard to identify where Jerusalem ends and Judea begins. The same difficulty is true in identifying clear boundaries between Judea and Samaria.

Perhaps our Jerusalems involve, first, the inner world already discussed. Jerusalem for us may also include our immediate families and more distant relatives.

Judea might pick up where Jerusalem left off, with our close friends as well as neighbors.

Samaria goes beyond. It could include our everyday acquaintances and persons we meet in everyday experiences.

Look specifically at our Jerusalems. Since we have already

dealt with the inner world, pick up with our immediate families.

As we move beyond ourselves, family members are persons we probably come in contact with most frequently. However, this situation is not always true.

How well do you know your family, and how extended is your family tree?

My family might be considered small. I am single and live alone. When I have my shoes on in the morning and am ready to walk out the door for the day, everyone in my family is ready. Yes, I am a family unit of one. But my family really involves more than myself. It includes my father and mother, sister, brother, and their families.

My definition of immediate family includes those I am in contact with frequently. I talk with at least one member of my family once or twice a week, even though they live in separate cities. Immediate family usually includes those persons living under one roof. But the immediate family is certainly not limited to that particular group of persons.

I have often thought how much easier it is to share my feelings and beliefs with friends and other persons than with family members. Even though I consider my family close, it is sometimes hard to share my deepest feelings with them. Why? Perhaps the reason is that they know me best. My mother insists that she can tell over the telephone exactly the kind of day I have had. Her evaluation is not based on what I have said, but the way I have said it. She probably knows me better than any other person.

I am convinced that a consistent witness in the outer world must first start with a consistent, open relationship within one's immediate family. Having the best possible relationship within the family is essential. Establishing this positive relationship starts in realizing that the family is not perfect.

Perhaps the hardest but most freeing part of becoming an adult is realizing that our parents are not perfect. They make mistakes. I believe that most parents do the best they can, based on their knowledge and skills at the time, in raising their children in a loving and nurturing environment. Yet such environments do not always seem loving and nurturing.

Many adults still live lives of defeat. They spend much of

their loving energy blaming their parents and their past for the present. How often have you heard these words? "My parents put me down." "They got me off to a bad start." "It's not my fault that I turned out like this." If we are to discover our witness, we must discover peace and forgiveness within our families. We must not pursue the past in order to blame others for our problems.

Therapists find validity in looking at one's past family experiences to determine present actions and tendencies. However, we are responsible for who we are. So what if we grew up in a nonperfect family? If you identify with that statement, you join the ranks of most other human beings.

Families are not perfect, but they are God's model for a healthy emotional and spiritual life. God gave us the home as a context in which we learn to build relationships. The home is a personal lab for life in which we learn reconciliation. When this reconciliation happens, our winning witness can begin to expand. Such peaceful relationships begin by meeting the needs of those in our immediate families.

My sister, Teresa, is the finest example I know of one who meets needs within our family. Seldom does a week pass that she does not call, drop a note, or encourage one of her three children to call or write Aunt Bobbish (my family name).

What responsibility do I have in meeting the needs of my parents, brother, sister, and their families? I have a responsibility to be loving. So often I find the real me coming out more when I am at home than anywhere else. I am not always loving, giving, and unselfish with family members. If I cannot be consistent in a loving relationship with my family, how can I develop a winning, consistent, loving relationship outside of those who know and love me most?

I also have the responsibility to listen. I am sure that if I were married and had children of my own, I would have more opportunity to be a listener. But when I am with my immediate family, I should take every opportunity to listen to what they say and what they do not say. Sometimes what we feel is their need may not be their need at all. Only by listening through the Father's ears can I hear. It is only then that I can respond to their needs.

My Jerusalem also includes other relatives. If you are like me, you may not know all of your relatives. You may even need to subdivide your relatives into close relatives and distant relatives. My close relatives include my grandparents and Aunt Loyce. All live within one hour from me. My distant relatives include many aunts and uncles living in cities far away. I have what seems to be an infinite network of cousins. I have not seen many of them in years.

Aunt Loyce had a family celebration not too many months ago. Since I live nearby, I had a chance to go and become reacquainted with many relatives whom I had not seen in years. While I felt I did not really know them, I sensed kinship. There was a bond. As I drove home from the extended family gathering, I thought about each person and his or her personal life and needs. I had to ask myself, What am I doing, or what could I do, to make a difference in their lives? I was surprised with my answers. I could pray for them specifically. I could write notes and ask them about their needs, sharing my own needs with them. Keeping in touch would certainly help in praying for them specifically. I could live up to my family name by maintaining a supportive contact. Such contacts certainly might not be as frequent as in my immediate family, but a personal contact is essential in making a difference in our extended family world.

As I think about my own Jerusalem—my immediate and extended family—I must also consider the questions, Which family members are Christians? Can I list them by name?

I must be available to God to be used to establish a consistent, loving, and supportive relationship in order to make a difference in the lives of my relatives. This difference comes as I first make myself available to them. Being available might start by an action as simple as sending a Valentine or Christmas card to Aunt Ola Mae in California, or giving Grandma a surprise visit, and saying, "I just wanted to tell you that I love you."

I may not be able to win every member of my family to Christ. But I can make a winning difference in their lives.

What about Judea? Look again at Thompson's illustration to determine that our Judeas may include close friends and neighbors.

First, friendship. Sometimes I feel that my friends are my family. It is hard to separate the two, especially since I live miles from my nearest relative.

What is a close friend? Like family members, a close friend is one whom I love unconditionally and who loves me unconditionally. "A friend loveth at all times" (Prov. 17:17). What does it mean to make friendships and to be a friend? Why is it that some people seem to be constantly surrounded by friends while others seem to have so few? Ultimately, to have friends we must be a friend. The following questions about friendship will help us understand more clearly the meaning of friendship:

• Do I view my relationships with friends as a two-way street?

• Do I compare my friends with each other? Or accept each one as a person of worth even though her values, appearance, and life-style may be different from others?

• Do I accept the fact that I do not have to be everything to everybody at all times?

• Do I allow my friends to seek my advice? Or do I feel the overwhelming need to be the do-gooder and give advice regardless of my friends' perception of their needs?

• Do I accept my friends as they really are? Or do I make demands that they change as a condition for continuing our relationship?

• Do I seek to broaden my circle of friendships, or do I limit myself to only one or two significant others?

• Do I feel close enough to my friends to really be me? (Being me means sharing Christ within, consistently.) Or do I feel that in order to be accepted by such friends, I must adjust who I am to fit their expectations?

• Do my friendships maintain a spiritual balance? Do I discuss that which is most important to us and does that discussion include my relationship to Jesus Christ?

• Do I allow my friendships space? Or am I often tempted to be overly curious and overstep their need for privacy?

• Do I maintain in confidence what is shared with me by my friends in confidence?

• Do I treat my friends as responsible and independent persons?

• Do I avoid the temptation to straighten out my friends? Or do I yield to the temptation to help them to know all that I perceive is wrong with them?[2]

Friendships are key in developing a winning witness. Often "our relationship with a friend who is hurting may enable us to help when someone who is more skilled could not."[3]

True, meaningful friendships are the music of life. Do your friendship skills need tuning?

Sometimes neighbors are our friends. If your life-style is like mine, however, you may not even know your neighbor's name. According to Thompson, this section of our Judea can also include business associates and extended friendships, such as school friends. These persons are ones with whom we do not keep in close touch or do not consider to be "significant others."

I often wonder if my neighbors even know I am a Christian. Many of them do not even know my name as I do not know theirs. But I am still responsible for them. They are included in my outer world.

Not too many weeks ago I noticed at least 15 cars parked in front of a neighbor's house. I learned later there had been a death in the family. I wish I had responded. Times of joy or grief are perfect times to make an initial and lasting contact with a neighbor.

I do know one of my neighbors—Dave.

Each morning before the sun hits the pavement, my tennis shoes are out the front door. My neighborhood is one that is physically fit! After two or three weeks of the routine, I began to recognize the same faces. The consistency made it comfortable to at least speak and acknowledge that we were all dedicated to the same thing—fitness. One time I left town for a three-week trip. On my first morning out after the trip, Dave stopped jogging, introduced himself, and said, "Where have you been? I have been missing you. I thought maybe you were sick or something." I explained that I had been away on a business trip. This conversation opened the opportunity to share what I did and what he did for a living. Dave's closing remark that day was, "Don't dare leave town again without telling some of us. We can at least check the mail and not worry!"

Since that time, Dave and his wife, Margie, have become real neighborhood friends. I am looking forward to having them over one evening to further develop this friendship. Who knows? Dave and Margie may not be Christians. Maybe

I am the one to make a difference in their lives.

As we move away from Judea we enter our Samarias. Samaria could include our acquaintances and the person Thompson calls Person X.

Who are our acquaintances? Remember the encounter at the beginning of this chapter? Acquaintances may include those persons you do not know but who seem to come into your life frequently.

Think about your routines. How often do you use the same teller at the bank, grocery store, or post office?

Establishing a relationship with acquaintances comes first by recognizing them. I believe we are the ones to take the initiative. Many acquaintances mentioned above wear name tags. Watch their faces when you greet them with a smile as you call them by name. You can be sure that they will make a mental note of you because you recognized them. By recognizing them you have established and communicated that you feel they are important. Establishing a winning witness that counts with acquaintances can start by communicating your feelings of their self-worth.

Finally, there is Person X. I meet them often. They are the persons who are on airplanes, in hotels, in restaurants, and other places that I may not frequent. A LIVINGtouch witness can still happen with nonfrequent relationships. Often we use the excuse that they are someone else's responsibility. After all, they belong to someone else's family and are someone else's friend. But that someone else may not have your conviction about celebrating a life-style that could make a difference in their world. Yes, we are responsible for Person X.

I travel a lot. Travel is a perfect opportunity for me to communicate Christ's love in small ways. I always remember this when I leave the tip. I try to call the waitress by name and I try to treat her or him as an equal, and not as my servant.

I have a friend who practices leaving her tip inside a small tract that explains God's plan of salvation. I think this is a remarkable idea. But such actions must be consistent with the prior actions. If we have been rude, or inconsistent, the tract and tip will be considered a hypocrisy and may be more damaging than good.

I believe in what Oscar Thompson calls "holy magnetism." When we concentrate on winning our outer world for Christ, people are drawn to us.

I have a theory. It is not based on evidence, or theological study. My theory is this: you do not have to go fishing to win the lost. You simply need to launch your boat. The fish will usually jump in.

THE CHALLENGE TO TOUCH
Part 1: Identifying the Lost

How well are you in touch with your outer world? Use the graph below to help put names or faces of lost persons with each group. Write the name of at least one person you know in each group who does not know Jesus Christ as Saviour.

GROUPS IN EXTERNAL WORLD	NAMES OF PERSONS
Immediate Family	
Relatives	
Close Friends	
Neighbors/business associates	
Acquaintances	
Person X	

Part 2: Winning the Lost

What can you do today, tomorrow, or this month to strengthen relationships in each group? Plan specific actions to touch the lives of the persons in each group. If you do not know a non-Christian, do not be devastated. Use this exercise as a reminder to get acquainted with one. Write in the space provided specific ways you can do this today, tomorrow, and this month. First, copy the names you listed in part 1 in the left column on the next page. Second, write specific actions. You may wish to review pages 73-82 for suggestions.

NAMES OF LOST PERSONS	MY PLAN TO WITNESS TODAY, TOMORROW, THIS MONTH

---

[1]W. Oscar Thompson, Jr., and Carolyn Thompson, *Concentric Circles of Concern* (Nashville: Broadman Press, 1981), 21. All rights reserved. Used by permission.

[2]Donna Maples, *Friends Are for Helping* (Birmingham: New Hope, 1986), 16-20.

[3]Ibid., 15.

7
Overcoming Barriers and Obstacles

"I can do everything through Him who gives me strength"
(Phil. 4:13 NIV).

THE TOUCH: THE ENCOUNTER WITH OLGA

The flight left at midnight Alabama time. I was tired, spent, and eager to get home. It would be 12 to 15 hours before the final leg of the trip from Anchorage, Alaska, ended at the Birmingham airport. But it was a good tired. I felt the week of leading seminars, speaking, and consulting had been well worth it. As usual, I seemed to be the one that received the greatest blessing!

Though I needed rest, it was difficult to sleep on the plane. We made stops and changed planes in nearly every airport from Portland eastward.

It was midway through the trip, in Dallas, that I boarded the last plane of the journey. There I met Olga.

She was bundled in a blanket and glued to a paperback book when I first noticed her. My seat was next to hers. She did not notice me. While I was not exactly alert, I could not help but see that Olga was different.

Either my curiosity, or caffeine from numerous cups of coffee served on the flight, had me fully awake by then. I did not want to stare, but Olga had gotten my attention.

"I wonder what nationality she is," I thought. "Maybe I can get a clue if I can see what she's reading."

Very inconspicuously, I glanced at her book. Before I realized it, I had already asked, "Can you actually read that?" It looked foreign—Russian, perhaps.

She dropped the book and said frankly in her broken English, "No! I am just looking at the pages to impress people like you!"

I felt awful. Talk about getting off to a bad start!

"I'm sorry. I hope you will accept my apology. Of course I know you can read it. You see, I am just impressed. I mean, I don't even speak perfect English much less any other language. I do hope you will forgive my lack of sensitivity. Let me introduce myself. I'm Marsha Spradlin."

"I'm Olga. Really, it's OK. I am used to people staring and asking questions. It's been that way all of my life."

I was puzzled. I did not know how to respond. Should I pursue the conversation or should I just let her get back to her book? After a moment, I realized she was waiting for me to respond.

"Oh, so you have lived here all of your life?"

"Oh, no! My life story is far more complicated than that," she explained.

She was right. During the next hour and a half she unfolded her remarkable life story.

I clung to every word. First, her English was difficult to understand. And second, her life story was incredible.

Olga grew up in a wealthy Russian family. Her father was a Russian official. His responsibilities included engineering the Amazon Dam in South America. Olga moved to South America with her family while still in her teens. It was there that she first experienced rejection and prejudice.

"No one accepted a Russian, especially not there and then!"

Unrest broke out while the family was in South America. Olga's father was the target of a political conspiracy. The story was terrifying, especially the night her home was vandalized and both parents murdered. Olga and her two younger brothers escaped.

"That was when I learned something of responsibility. I was the oldest, but still a child. Someone had to take care of my brothers. We fled for our lives as we sought refuge." How they survived the months on the run was itself a story.

The three children did survive and found their own hiding place where they spent the next several years. Olga got a job doing cleaning. This job provided enough money to buy food and pay for a tiny shelter.

During that time she met Frank, a military man from the United States. Frank was of another race, but skin color had no meaning to Olga. Acceptance, trust, and love did.

In 1984 Frank's tour of duty was completed. He and Olga had been married for six years and had adopted two children, one black and one white. They moved to San Antonio, Frank's home.

"Marsha, no one there wanted to be our friends because we were so different. Frank is a wonderful father, and I love him and my children. But I would love to have a friend."

While I did not want to miss a word, my heart was in the midst of self-examination. My ears continued to listen while my heart asked some deep and painful questions: Is this a coincidence? Or am I to be that friend? What about my own prejudices? Am I prejudiced?

I was not comfortable with my answers. But I was comfortable with what I knew to be true.

I knew Olga was not on my flight only because she was scheduled to meet Frank in Atlanta. She was there because God had so engineered the course of events in our lives that our hearts should touch. The encounter was God's plan. The choice of how I would respond to her was mine.

Frank had been transferred to the South. They were meeting in Atlanta to investigate options for housing and schools for the children.

"We will move to the South in a month, Marsha. Will they accept us?"

I could not respond. I knew the answer. Probably not!

At no time during our conversation did Olga mention God. I knew what I had to do. He could well be the only One Who could fully love, accept, and provide the friendship and refuge she was seeking.

"Olga, I am not sure about how well you and Frank will be accepted when you move. But I am sure about one thing. I do know where and Who can give you the love and friendship, not to mention the acceptance."

Olga's painful life caused her heart to be open. She clung to my every word as I explained to her Who God is, where He is, why He sent His Son Jesus to redeem us from all sin, and how He could be our Source of strength and refuge. Apparently, no one had ever introduced her to Jesus Christ before.

The plane landed in Atlanta. I was scheduled to make connections to Birmingham, and Olga was to meet Frank. I knew we would probably never see each other again. I knew also that the seed of hope had been planted. And I knew more than anything my need to seek forgiveness for the prejudices in my life, about which I had not even been aware, that could block an effective witness.

I gave Olga my address. I never heard from her again. Yet somehow I believe we will meet again.

Challenging the Barriers and Obstacles

I am more convinced than ever that we often miss such bright encounters because of fear, lack of awareness, feelings of incompetence to identify with persons different from ourselves, and the simple lack of being available.

Fear is one of the more obvious obstacles blocking the joy of bright encounters. Fear could be defined as a camouflage of excuses for why we do not witness. Each of us could probably list 101 reasons why we cannot witness. No doubt you agree that these reasons are a cover. Underneath the cover is fear.

Fear is simply being afraid of the unknown. It might be well to remember that fear has never been uncommon. In glancing through the concordance in my Bible, I located 70 references to fear. Why is there so much talk about fear in the Scriptures? The answer is not unlike the answer we would give for being afraid to witness or to represent Jesus Christ. We are afraid of opposition. It is easier to give in to fear than to face it and overcome it.

What is fear? I have heard it described as false information appearing real. This description may be true. While there are many forms of fear, four forms seem obvious as we prepare to be winning witnesses: the fear of change, the fear of failure, the fear of success, and the fear of opposition.

Look at each fear. The fear of change is not uncommon. We all feel uneasy about the unknown. Often such fear is not real—it is our perception that is the problem. Yet change may feel like a disturbing intruder. It leaves us with only the choice of how to respond.

Does the word *change* cause butterflies inside you? Do you have a deep-down panic when you think of change because of your desire to keep things the way they are? If we are going to be serious about being witnesses, some changes will need to be made in our life-styles.

For many persons, change means moving away from their comfort zone. We find comfort in the certainties of our past even though our past track records may not be successful. Likewise, we tend to panic as we anticipate the future, even though the future could be brighter and more positive.

Instead of viewing change as negative, why not think of it as neutral or even better, a positive word? Think of change as growth, choices, development, and challenge. By no means do I wish to imply that changing your life-style is easy. But such a change can be done when we concentrate on the results. The process of change falls into place when we focus on the results.

A friend of mine once said, "Marsha, do you know how you can have anything in the world?" Curiosity overwhelmed me.

"Easy!" she said. "Simply never forget what you want."

All too often we focus our attention on the process of change. We seem to become overwhelmed with the steps and the time involved in change, not to mention the setbacks we experience as we seek change. We must focus on the end result.

The fear of failure can destroy your witness. This fear comes as we concentrate on past experiences and project them into the future. I remember a personal witnessing encounter which was a total flop. I felt rejected. Suddenly it occurred to me that it was not me that was rejected, but Jesus Christ. My responsibility was to tell the good news. Securing results is not a part of my job description. The fear of failure can immobilize us.

The fear of success is another fear that is often not obvious. What if we are successful? Does success mean more change in our life-styles and more responsibility? The fear of opposition is a third fear. Face it. The world is occupied by Satan. Evangelism persuades those held by Satan to recognize Jesus as their Lord. The prince of this world will resist this change. As we speak the good news we must be ready to oppose him. Read Acts 4:1-31 for insights into how Peter and John handled opposition from the religious leaders of their day.

The Pharisees received a lot of bad press. While they may have had more in common with Jesus than any other group of His time, they were still His severest critics. They were separatists and were devoted to maintaining the Levitical laws of purity (Luke 18:12; Matt. 23:23). They became stereotyped in many ways because of their elaborate ceremonial code. Many of Jesus' followers were intimidated and afraid of confrontation. They were different. We still find it hard today to identify and care for persons who are different.

Fear causes us to become POWs (prisoners of our own world), not to mention prisoners of ourselves. In order to overcome the barriers of fear, we must be freed from the fear of persons who are different from ourselves. We must be willing to face the truth about ourselves. What are you afraid of?

Lack of vision may be the second obstacle keeping us from capturing bright encounters.

I remember as a fifth-grader the experience of getting glasses for the first time. I had been diagnosed as having myopia, the inability to see things far away. I shall never forget the drive home from the eye doctor after getting my first pair of glasses. I noticed the crisp leaves on the trees. Each leaf was individually arranged. They had been there all along, but my visual handicap had prevented me from noticing them.

I wonder if we as Christians lack in our personal witnessing opportunities because of spiritual myopia. We see our own needs, those close up. Yet we are unable to see sharply the needs of others.

Likewise, how many of us lack a witness due to spiritual

presbyopia, the inability to see needs nearby? Presbyopia is the direct opposite of myopia. How often do we see needs of others across the waters, yet miss the needs of persons living in our own household, neighborhood, or church?

How do we get a vision for the lost? Always meditate upon the knowledge of the needs of the world and the saving grace of Christ. Keep that truth with you day and night and as time passes God will enable you to share it more and more.

A vision includes seeing things as they really are. In *Discovering the Depths*, William Clemmons described Jesus' concern regarding vision. He said Jesus was concerned with His disciples' ability to see. He would end a discourse with the words, "He who has eyes to see, let him see," or "He who has ears to hear, let him hear." But Jesus knew having eyes and ears did not guarantee that a person would know what was occurring in the world. Are we really seeing the world as lost?

I recently taught a personal witnessing seminar at one of the larger churches in our city. The Wednesday evening service had about 175 in attendance.

I asked the question, How many of you know a lost person?

Of the 175 persons, only 3 raised their hands.

I was stunned!

Before we can win the world for Christ, we must become aware of the lostness of the world.

Ability is a third obstacle which keeps us from missing a bright encounter. Not only is witnessing a skill, it is the ability to walk in someone else's moccasins. Likewise, witnessing is the ability to walk in our own moccasins as we take a realistic look in identifying the skills and abilities we need to become that witness.

Ability to witness lies first in discovering the gift of caring. Most people struggle not to be self-centered. Rather than that, perhaps humans should strive to become other-centered. We will further explore gifts and skills in chapters 8 and 9.

Availability is closely tied to ability. It communicates that we really care. It is central to the Christian witness. I am convinced that we have two purposes for existing: to be available to have a personal relationship with Jesus Christ, and to be available to serve others through personal encounters and relationships. But how often do we get so caught up in our routine of everydayness that we lack the ability to be available? We become so busy doing that we fail to be.

Oscar Thompson insists that "the most important word in the English language, apart from proper nouns, is *relationship*."[1] How available are we?

Time often becomes the barrier which blocks our availability, or at least it seems to be a legitimate excuse. How often have you said, "I would do more if I just had time." Or have you ever wished for a 34-hour day? Why do we feel that more time would relieve the pressure under which we live? No doubt, even if we had more time, we would soon be as frustrated as we are in a 24-hour-day allotment.

In his article, "Tyranny of the Urgent," Charles Hummel puts the urgent and the important in perspective. He challenges us to examine our priorities, to avoid letting urgent matters displace the truly important ones. "The problem is that the most important tasks rarely must be done today or even this week . . . these projects can wait. But the urgent task calls for instant action . . . endless demands pressure every hour and day."[2]

To be a LIVINGtouch witness we must not become victims of time. We cannot afford to lose today by looking at the past, or even the future. We must look directly into the now and ask ourselves, What can I do now to make a difference in my world?

Communication can be a barrier, but it can also be viewed as an amazing resource for sharing the gospel. Think about it. The ability to communicate is far more fascinating and complicated than most of us realize. The fact that you can read the symbols—called words—printed on this page and comprehend and interpret their meaning is incredible.

For communication to occur, there must be three factors: a message, a sender, and a receiver. The message is Jesus Christ. We are called to be the senders. The lost world is the target audience to receive the message. But there is still another important ingredient in communication—the way in which the message is sent. The way communication is packaged often influences if or how well the receiver receives the message. Past experiences, culture, background, and even age, are factors to consider when identifying the "package" you wish to use in communicating your message. The message may be the same, but the way you send it must vary, depending on your audience.

I remember a childhood experience in which a well-meaning minister presented the gospel in symbolic terms. As an eight-year-old, I walked down the church aisle because I thought I was supposed to. I did not understand the minister's words, "If you give your heart to Jesus, you'll be washed in the blood, and when you die you will sit on God's right hand." I had visions of blood, and hearts, and sitting on God's hand after I died. It was not a conversion experience. That experience came later for me. I had not received the message in words that made sense to me. Instead, I had interpreted the minister's words in symbolic language and had responded out of fear to that message.

To be a LIVINGtouch witness, we must consider communication as one of the most important tools for sharing Christ. But, lest we be too concerned, remember that the Holy Spirit is the ultimate communicator for convicting hearts and interpreting the message. What a relief!

THE CHALLENGE TO TOUCH

Take a moment to identify why your witness may not have been effective in the past. Review pages 87-92. Write below the fears and barriers described on these pages that seem to be an obstacle which prevents you from witnessing. For example, have you been plagued with fear; lack of awareness; lack of ability; or refusal to be available because of time or skill; or an inability to communicate? Be honest with yourself. List your fears here:

What steps will you take to overcome the fears and barriers you identified above? Write each fear in the space provided below. Next to each one, write a sentence that describes how you plan to overcome each obstacle. Remember, we "can do all things though Christ who strengthens" us!

---

[1]W. Oscar Thompson, Jr., and Carolyn Thompson, *Concentric Circles of Concern* (Nashville: Broadman Press, 1981), 13.

[2]The 2:7 Series, 3d printing (Colorado Springs: Navpress, 1979), 21.

8
Determining His Goals and Seeking His Direction

"Not that I have already obtained all this, or have already been made perfect, but I press on to take hold of that for which Christ Jesus took hold of me. Brothers, I do not consider myself yet to have taken hold of it. But one thing I do: Forgetting what is behind and straining toward what is ahead, I press on toward the goal to win the prize for which God has called me heavenward in Christ Jesus" (Phil. 3:12-14 NIV).

THE TOUCH: THE ENCOUNTER WITH JAMIE

The doorbell chimed.

Even though I was expecting her, I was startled as I opened the door and she plunged a gift into my hand.

"Surprise!" she said enthusiastically.

"Jamie, I invited you for coffee. Why are you gifting me?" I asked.

"I couldn't resist. It's coffee. Two kinds in fact. It's to celebrate the two years we've been neighbors."

As we chatted Jamie looked around my apartment. We joked and laughed and enjoyed coffee and muffins.

It was a perfect first visit. Even though we had been neighbors for two years, today was our first "official" visit. It was a victory for me. I had been planning such a visit for months. You might say it was a goal accomplished.

While this initial visit was a first, it was not to be the last.

Yet it may have been one of the most significant. It was during those first moments together that we established a foundation on which a deep, nurturing friendship eventually developed. This unique friendship developed to what I later called a "touchpoint," a point at which our hearts touched through Jesus Christ. Such points of contact make it possible for us to share our faith through ministry and witness. The content leads us to a point of sharing what God has done in our lives. For Jamie and me, the touchpoint came as I was able later to share with her God's plan of salvation.

But the sharing did not happen overnight. Jamie had lived two doors down my street for a couple of years. It was hard not to notice her. She was one of the most attractive women I had ever seen. For months we simply exchanged smiles and good mornings as she walked her Great Dane.

I thought often, "Who is this woman?" Apparently she did not work, nor did she have to. She drove an expensive late model car, wore beautiful clothes and unique jewelry, and always seemed up and charming. But somehow, deep within, I felt she was lonely, troubled, and hurting.

I shared my concern for Jamie with my friend, Barb. Barb, being the personal witnessing life-style type said, "Make her your own personal project, Marsh! I mean, set some goals. Think of some ways to get to know her. Go for it. What you may be feeling about Jamie may be a direct message from the Holy Spirit."

I thought about Barb's advice. I decided to go for it. Set goals? What kind of goals? I struggled with ways to meet Jamie. Then I decided to observe her life-style patterns.

Each morning she walked the dog between 6:00-6:30 A.M. "That's a good time to go for my morning walk," I thought. She never had company, except for one gentleman who would come by on rare occasions. She never left the complex except for Monday nights. She was always at home on Sunday morning. Obviously she did not attend church.

I determined first that my main contact would have to be between 6:00-6:30 A.M. as she walked the dog. Each morning before the sun was up I was starting my walk. At first it was simply, "Good morning." This pattern went on for months. Finally, I observed that she received a newspaper.

Usually the paper boy missed, so I made it a habit to pick up the paper and place it in front of the door.

Needless to say, Jamie began to wonder who was hand delivering the newspaper. One morning she caught me red handed.

"I just hate to see these in the middle of the driveway. You never know when you're going to back out of the driveway and wipe out the front page."

"I've been wondering who has been doing this. Thank you!"

"My name is Marsha Spradlin. That's quite a dog you have there."

"Yea, she's probably my best friend." Jamie looked at the Great Dane, "Mattie, this is Marsha!"

"Glad to meet you, Mattie," I said. "I rarely talk to dogs. Do they really understand people?"

"Mattie does!" Jamie insisted.

"I'm glad to meet you, Jamie. You too, Mattie. Better go now. Got to get to work. Hey, see you around."

For the following several weeks, Jamie and I exchanged good mornings in a little more personal way.

"Good morning, Marsha!"

"Good morning, Jamie! Looks like a great day!"

"Hope yours is special, Marsha."

This sort of conversation went on for months, finally over a year. Then summer came. I noticed Jamie packing her car as I went for an evening stroll. "Going on a vacation? I'd be glad to pick up your mail," I yelled, as I passed by her house.

"No, not really a vacation, but a trip. I am going down to Austin to pick up my girls. They have a few days off, and we've decided to spend a few days at Corpus in the sun!"

"Oh, you have children?"

"Yes, two darling girls. I'll have to show you their pictures sometime."

"Well, if they look anything like their mother, they are gorgeous."

"Oh, you're too nice, Marsha."

"They must be in college at the University of Texas."

"One is, but the other lives with her dad. We're divorced."

"Oh, Jamie, I'm sorry. I know that must be hard not having your kids and all."

"Hard! That's an understatement. I am a total failure as a mother. Otherwise, I would have my own kids!"

"Well, for now, Jamie, I hope every moment with them is fantastic. Be careful driving down. When you get back, I want to see those pictures!"

"It's a deal."

After that short conversation, I determined that I was right. Inside that beautiful woman was one tormented by failure, limitations, and a lack of a relationship with the Father. Jamie was in pain.

I prayed for Jamie all weekend. On Monday, I watched for her car. I hoped to be available when she returned. It was Tuesday before we met again. It was early, before sunrise.

I greeted Jamie and after sharing hellos we made plans to meet for brunch on Saturday. That was the day she arrived at my door with a gift of coffee.

That Saturday morning's visit was the first of a series. In fact, we enjoyed being together so much that we decided to make Saturday morning brunch a habit. It was a positive addition to our lives.

It took months before I really felt I knew Jamie. But like the cocoon from which emerges a butterfly, she came out of her solitude. She began to trust her feelings and emotions with me, her new friend.

I learned that in order to bring out the best in Jamie, I had to be willing to be vulnerable myself. Being vulnerable meant sharing not just my strengths, but my own fears, mistakes, and incompetencies.

After a couple of months of Saturday brunches at my place, Jamie invited me into her home for the 10:00 A.M. talk time. It was my first visit in her home. I was overwhelmed. The delicious smell was not blueberry muffins and coffee, but homemade cinnamon rolls. Jamie, a gourmet cook, was amazing. Her kitchen cabinets reminded me of a familiar television cooking show. She had every kitchen gadget available. Her spice rack was a collection unlike anything I had ever seen. My being impressed did not stop in the kitchen. Her home was decorated beautifully with imported oriental rugs and ornate lamps, as well as extraordinary furnishings.

"Jamie, why haven't you invited me earlier? This place is absolutely awesome!"

Jamie laughed as she suggested that "stuff" really did not have meaning to her.

Personally, I agreed, but I certainly did not object to having nice things!

Our visit in Jamie's home was by far more special than any previous visit. Maybe the comfort of her own setting led her to open herself up to me more than ever. During the hours together that morning I learned about the real Jamie, the Jamie that was divorced because her husband had finally recognized her closet drug and alcohol addiction. That was the reason she lost her children. She had spent time in a mental hospital for chemical dependency.

"No judge in the state of Texas will give custody to such a mother," Jamie explained.

"I don't know how it got started," she went on. "Slowly, I guess. I kept a cover for years. I would hide the booze in suitcases, closets, and medicine bottles. I knew I was getting worse, but I couldn't cope. I had no one. I was too proud to admit I was a fake and a failure. After all, it would have been so destructive to Jim's reputation.

"You see, Jim, my ex-husband, was an outstanding physician in Houston. That's where we lived then. We were known as the perfect family. I was the perfect wife. Our kids were the perfect kids. Our home was the biggest and the best. But, something was missing—Jim. He was never home. Calls in the middle of the night got old. After 20 years of waking up without a partner, I realized I didn't have a marriage. But I had plenty of things.

"Bad got worse when I realized that the girls didn't need me anymore. I can see now that they really did. I just didn't see it then. They developed their own friends. They simply grew up. I tried to hold on to them. That's when I started having severe problems with them. They didn't want to be at home. I caved in. I craved help. We had always had liquor in the house, a wet bar. It was the easiest way to escape. It got out of hand.

"Jim found me unconscious one afternoon. Being a physician, well, he knew what he had on his hands. A drunk.

"I was admitted into the hospital. I tried. I really tried, Marsha, and after months of rehabilitation I was released on an outpatient basis. You would think that things would then be better. They weren't. That's when the fear set in. I developed agoraphobia."

"Agrophi . . . what?" I asked.

"It's an emotional illness. It means you can't leave the house. For nearly two years I couldn't go anywhere. Jim nearly went nuts. In addition to his practice and the demands at work, he now had to do all the grocery shopping. We never entertained friends as before. That's when he asked for a divorce. I wasn't who he married, he said.

"Again, I entered a mental treatment center. I stayed for four months. The divorce came through during that time. When I was released, it was advised that I make some changes in my environment. One change was to move. After all, Jim and I were divorced. That's when I moved to Dallas.

"Slowly, I regained the ability to at least go to the grocery store. Moving was about the most difficult thing I had ever experienced. That's why I am here in Dallas.

"Jim has been good to me. He still sponsors me financially and calls on occasions. In fact, he bought this house. I am still under constant medical and psychiatric care, and I am involved in the local chapter of Alcoholics Anonymous. We meet on Monday nights at the Marriott. I guess they are my closest friends.

"Pete and Kate, you may have seen their car here before, are my sponsors. They check on me once a week and, if I get into trouble, I call them. They are alcoholics too. Part of the rehabilitation is to eventually become someone else's sponsor. You are never cured from alcoholism. It's a daily fight. Once an alcoholic, always an alcoholic.

"I can't believe I have told you all of this. You must now think I am awful. I don't blame you if you never want to have anything to do with me again."

"No, Jamie. In fact, I believe I love you more this moment than ever before. I believe it is only by God's grace that others haven't had the same kind of problems. An addiction as an escape could happen to anyone, including me."

I reached out and touched her hands. Squeezing them, I said, "I love you. Will you let me be your friend? The kind that supports and prays for you. When you have a hard day, you can tell me. I want to be here for you."

Jamie started to cry. "I want a friend, Marsha. I want to say yes, but I don't want you involved in this mess."

"Let's take it one day at a time. OK?"

One day at a time was what we did.

Days passed before I saw Jamie again. I felt she was avoiding me. I could understand why she would. She had been so vulnerable. I guess she felt embarrassed. I decided if ever she needed to know that she had a consistent friend it was now. How could I express my unconditional love?

Ah, I could send her flowers. I did just that and included a note. "I love you, friend. Brunch on Saturday? My place, 10:00 A.M. sharp. RSVP."

Jamie left a note on my door indicating her gratitude for the flowers and that she would keep our brunch tradition.

Our friendship began to take on a whole new dimension.

I traveled a lot, which was hard for Jamie at first. She was lonely. While I knew not to allow her to become dependent, I felt I had to let the Father handle that possibility. I must be available. That was my deepest knowledge of the Father's will. How could I be available, build trust, and still travel?

As I spent time with the Father daily, I began to jot down goals, both short-term and long-term goals. My short-term goals included leaving Jamie my travel itinerary so that she could reach me in case of an emergency. Also I could leave my mailbox key with her. This act would let her know I trusted her. As our friendship and trust grew, Jamie got a key to the condo. She watered my plants, took care of my mail, and even packed little goodie bags with danishes and trail-mix for my long trips.

Long-term goals included giving Jamie a Bible, inviting her to church, and even going with her to an AA meeting. My ultimate goal was to share the plan of salvation with her.

Slowly, the goals became reality, not just dreams. However, we had much to experience before such goals were accomplished.

After a weekend trip, I stopped by Jamie's house to pick up my mail on the way home from the airport. She was sitting on her front porch with a blank stare.

"Jamie, are you alright?"

She laughed. "No, I'm stoned." Then she cried. "I got off

the wagon. Bad. I lost my keys. I can't get into the house."
"Quick! What do I do?" I thought.

After taking Jamie to my condo, I realized it was Monday night. Jamie always went to AA on Monday nights. I remembered Jamie telling me about the Marriott. I called and asked for Pete, her sponsor. He was there. I explained what I had found. He and Kate were there in minutes. They had a key to her house.

We sat up with Jamie most of the night. The night was not as bad as the next day. Jamie was so embarrassed. She had been "clean" for nearly a year. Now she had to start over. She was devastated.

"What caused it?" Pete asked.

"I was just lonely."

The following days were awkward, but we managed to share openly, as I tried to encourage Jamie. I knew her birthday was coming up. The birthday could be a perfect time for accomplishing a long-term goal!

I planned a birthday party for four: Jamie, Pete, Kate, and, of course, me. We had a meal, cake, the works. For a gift I gave Jamie a Bible. Inside I wrote:

I accept you like you are. I wish I could say I understand the pain you have now. But I don't. Yet, I know Who does. The Father. Let Him love you. You are so easy to love. He loves you already. I do too. Please accept my love by accepting this gift. Happy Birthday, friend!

Jamie accepted the gift. The next day she placed a gift at my door. It was a book. She had given me a copy of the devotional book for alcoholics. Inside was a note:

You gave to me your book. Here is mine. I will read yours. Will you read mine? Maybe we can talk about what we read.

Goals were being accomplished through His perfect timing. At our next Saturday's brunch we discussed our readings. We asked questions. We expressed our love.

"Marsha, will you go with me to AA next Monday?"

I could hardly believe what I was hearing.

"Yes! I would love to. Jamie, will you go with me to church on Sunday?"

"I have been wanting to, Marsha. Yes!"

For the next few months I attended Jamie's AA meetings

and she attended Sunday School and the worship service at my church with me. On the way home from each meeting we usually grabbed a bite to eat and discussed what we had learned.

AA was an education for me. The people at these meetings were some of the most supportive, loving people I had ever met. Likewise, Jamie began to feel loved and accepted by my friends at church. They sent her cards and welcomed her warmly.

At last the opportunity came.

"Marsha, I enjoy AA. I have to have it, but church is different. The people are different. I want to be a part of your people. I read your Bible every night. I think I know what to do. I think only God can give me peace and release me from my prison. Will you pray with me? Now!"

We did pray. Jamie became my sister in Christ. Deep inside I also prayed a prayer of gratitude: "Thank you Father, for Barb, who encouraged me to set goals. Such goals made the winning difference in Jamie's life."

Setting Goals

I am jolted out of bed by the clock radio at the same time each morning. I eat precisely at the same time each day. Twice a month I have a predetermined amount of money set aside for savings. Once or twice a month I complete reading one book on my "haven't read yet" shelf in my study. I have an idea of exactly what I want to weigh. I am committed to walking four miles a day. I spend the first minutes each morning in solitude, my quiet time in which only coffee, the Father's presence, and a few good books are allowed.

What do all of these unrelated life-style mannerisms have in common? In one way or another they each represent a goal. Where did they come from? Me! I have placed a premium on certain life-style actions. How did they become incorporated into my life-style? Through choice, dedication, conviction, discipline, and practice.

I am no expert in goal management. There are many persons who claim to be. Bookstore shelves are stacked with self-help books on how to set and maintain goals in nearly every area of life. There are books on how to pay for your home in five years, start a business, maintain the perfect weight, and keep a spiritual journal.

With such emphasis on goals in our society, I became interested in how goal setting could merge with our Christian witness. In my research on personal witnessing, I discovered that little, if any, attention was given to setting personal witnessing goals. The reason may be that we feel "that's the work of the Holy Spirit."

I thought about that reason, and researched the Scriptures. If goals play a significant role in a LIVINGtouch, I believe it is because of the direction from the Holy Spirit. Goal setting is not a new thing. While it may be a trend in today's society to accomplish more for me and mine, the Scriptures make it clear that goals are a part of the daily witness and life-style of a winner. Goal setting for the Christian has a different motivation. Instead of for me and mine, the motivation is for Thee and Thine.

The Scriptures are filled with examples of goal setting:
"On the third day I will reach my goal" (Luke 13:32 NIV).
"So we make it our goal to please Him" (2 Cor. 5:9 NIV).
"To attain your goal by human efforts" (Gal. 3:3 NIV).
"On toward the goal to win the prize" (Phil. 3:14 NIV).
"The goal of this command is love" (1 Tim. 1:5 NIV).
"For you are receiving the goal" (1 Peter 1:9 NIV).

Dig deeper with me:

Goals: What is a goal?

Webster defines the word *goal* as "the line or place at which a race, trip, etc., is ended. An object or end that one strives to attain; aim."[1]

While I seldom disagree with Webster, I would adjust his definition slightly. For Christians, goals are not simply the end, but the journey.

Do you remember the missions mandate recorded in Matthew 28:18-20? Take a minute to examine that key Scripture passage. Notice the goal-oriented words.

In order for these first-century Christians to achieve the remarkable success mandated in this Scripture passage—to make disciples—there had to be some goal setting.

Win and Charles Arn note in *The Master's Plan for Making Disciples*, "The goal was clear—make disciples. Being a disciple in the early church meant a firsthand involvement in the mission of Christ—making disciples. The goal was clear and all encompassing. An important facet of the early church's disciple-making goal was to continually expand this base of new disciples."[2]

One benefit of goal setting is the by-product. As we lead others to Jesus Christ, they become committed to the goal. They are then responsible themselves for continuing the disciple-making chain. New disciples are key instruments used by the Holy Spirit.

Think about your conversion experience. Can you remember a time when you were more excited about sharing what God had done in your life?

Goals: Who needs them?

I feel every believer needs clearly defined goals. The reason is outlined in Philippians 3:12-14. This Scripture passage makes it clear that we have not already obtained the goal yet, nor have we been made perfect. But with a goal we are able to at least get a grip or "to take hold" of His goal. His goal gives direction and incredible energy to press on.

Christians committed to making a LIVINGtouch difference in their world need a strategy. A direction. A goal! A tool to use to measure their progress. Without a goal, we are simply wandering with no specific direction.

Goals: Why set them?

Without goals we lack direction. We are not aware of where we are headed. Such unawareness leads to two things: We cannot know when we arrive and we become vulnerable to the winds of life. We can be easily blown off course. We become like a ship without a rudder.

By nature we are oriented toward the future. As Christians, we have the responsibility to think about the future of the people within our world. As we set goals and make people a priority in our lives, we develop direction.

Without direction, our Christian witness becomes aimless and nonspecific. We tend to escape responsibility for the lost.

Goals help us to filter out the cluttering messages that pull on our lives, our time, and our witness.

I do not want to communicate that as a Christian I always have clear direction in my life. As Christians we do not always know where we are going. That is faith. Goals simply grant direction and a vision. We do not need to know what we are going to do, just that God knows what to do.

If goal setting is so important, why do not we as Christians make goal setting more of a priority?

In Ted W. Engstrom's *A Time for Commitment*, he examines five reasons to ignore goal setting:

1. Friends can find you a lot faster when you're stuck in one place.
2. Co-workers won't have any trouble getting ahead of someone who's wandering in circles.
3. It's easier to procrastinate when there's less to put off.
4. Having no money saves time at the bank.
5. We can stop our list here. People without any goals don't accomplish much anyway.[3]

While not all of these reasons apply to the Christian witness, I think we can take each reason and apply it to our tendency to escape goal setting.

Why set goals? As Christians wanting to make a LIVINGtouch in the lives of others, we must identify what we want.

Goals: How do we set them?

"If you think a year ahead, sow a seed. If you think ten years ahead, plant a tree. If you think one-hundred years ahead, educate the people." Author Unknown

To be a witness we must first identify clearly what it is we want out of life. We want to be a LIVINGtouch witness. Therefore, we must think ahead. The further ahead we think, the better able we are to accomplish our goals. Remember that we are futuristic people. Thinking ahead does not mean we know the outcome. In fact, we cannot see the destination or outcome of 99 percent of our voyages. But as we think, we become.

It has been proven psychologically, and spiritually, that you become what you think about most. It is called your dominant thought. We tend to drift toward our most dominant thoughts. If you think about winning the world to Jesus

Christ, your actions follow. The Scriptures reinforce this: "Whatever is true, whatever is noble, whatever is right, whatever is pure, whatever is lovely, whatever is admirable—if anything is excellent or praiseworthy—think about such things" (Phil. 4:8 NIV).

Think about your personal goals.

• Selective forgetting. What could forgetting have to do with goal setting? Go back to the Philippians passage. "Brothers, I do not consider myself yet to have taken hold of it. But one thing I do: Forgetting what is behind and straining toward what is ahead, I press on toward the goal to win the prize for which God has called me heavenward in Christ Jesus" (Phil. 3: 14 NIV).

Part of establishing, maintaining, and reaching a goal includes forgetting. By concentrating on past mistakes and failure to reach our goals, we become immobilized. We become so overwhelmed with the baggage of the past that we are not free to look ahead. Such baggage uses energy. We lose our energy to press on. Goal setters never concentrate on past mistakes and failures except to use them as tools for learning.

• Knowing God. The most vital part of goal setting is establishing and maintaining an accurate knowledge and relationship with the One Who has given us the reason for the goal in the first place. Knowing how to set goals may be as simple as knowing God. However, there is a word of warning. In setting goals we cannot demand that God give direction. Even though we agree that the better we know Him, the better we can determine directions and goals in our lives, there are occasions when He is silent. Have you ever felt that you are desperately seeking His leadership, yet, He will not tell you what He is going to do or where or what you are to do? In those moments I have learned that He prefers that I simply concentrate on Who He is rather than what to do. As I concentrate patiently only on knowing Him, I learn not only what to do, but some rather incredible things about myself.

• Enjoying the journey. Often in goal setting we become so enchanted with the goals that we trip over them. We even miss the opportunity to accomplish the goal because our focus is only on the end result, not on the step-by-step process of reaching the goal. The joy of goal setting is the process or the journey. I have found this to be true in other areas of my Christian life as well. The journey must be moment by moment, day by day, in bits and pieces. The journey toward the accomplishment of the goal can be exhilarating. When we focus only on the end result we miss the joy of the process. The step-by-step process is grounded in determination and dedication. It is wrapped in flexibility, discipline, persistence, and balance.

Look at some step-by-step actions toward goal setting.

1. Set a long-range goal. What is it that you want to accomplish ultimately? Maybe your goal is to win a neighbor to the Father. Or maybe it is simply to meet your neighbor.

2. Set an intermediate goal. This goal may be called the long haul or the process. It is where the joy comes. It is usually the daily steps you identify that move you toward the end result. Give yourself specific times and limits to use to measure your progress toward these intermediate steps.

3. Set short-range goals. These goals are necessary stepping stones toward reaching the intermediate and long-range goals. A short-term goal could be simply learning a person's name.

4. Set goals that are just out of reach but not out of sight.

5. Get reinforcement by surrounding yourself with persons that share the value of your goals. They too are motivated individually to win their world to Christ. Become a support system and a prayer network.

6. Write down your goals. Review them daily. Get council from your support system when you seem to be off track.

7. Put your goals on index cards. Place them in strategic places in your home or office so that you see them often. These cards can become constant reminders of your goals and priorities.

8. Do not share your goals with negative people, those persons who might discourage your involvement. I remember clearly my feeling when trying to nurture Andrea. Some well-meaning friends insisted that I not get involved in her life. Listen to the Father, not others who might discourage you.

Goals: When do you set them?

Now is the only time there is. Yet while now is the start of setting goals, the actual direction may not come now! On occasion, I feel that I have blank spaces in my directions and goals. When God allows the open space, do not hurriedly attempt to fill it in. The space may be there to teach you what sanctification means, or what service means. Never run before God's leading. If there is the least bit of doubt, then He is not guiding. Whenever there is doubt, wait on the Lord.

Goals: Where do I start?

Start where you are. Do you remember Oscar Thompson's *Concentric Circles of Concern?* Thompson's concept may be a good exercise in getting started in a goal-setting strategy. Look at the grid below based on Thompson's *Concentric Circles.* Incorporate these circles into short-term, intermediate, and long-term goals. Since goals must be custom designed to fit your world, your life-style, and your gifts and abilities, only you can fill in the blank spaces. But, beware. Start by seeking the Father's leadership in the inner sanctuary of His divine presence.

Your goal setting may start with yourself. A long-term goal could be developing a witness. An intermediate goal could include thinking, reading, and saturating yourself in personal witnessing information; observing the life-style of a winning witness, a person whose witness is a LIVINGtouch example. A short-term goal could include establishing a relationship with a non-Christian. Use this process to fill in the spaces below.

	LONG-TERM	INTERMEDIATE	SHORT-TERM
Self			
Immediate family			
Relatives			
Friends			
Neighbors			
Acquaintances			
Person X			

108

THE CHALLENGE TO TOUCH

What did you learn about yourself after doing the exercise above? What actions will you take today to set goals and accomplish them? Tomorrow? Next month? Answer these questions: Do I need goals? Why should I set them? How do I set goals to win the world? When do I start? Where do I start? If you can answer these questions, what are you waiting for? Go for the goal!

---

[1]*Webster's New World Dictionary of the American Language*, 2d college ed., s.v. "goal."

[2]Win Arn and Charles Arn, *The Master's Plan for Making Disciples* (Pasadena: Church Growth Press, 1982), 21.

[3]Taken from *A Time of Commitment* by Ted W. Engstrom with Robert C. Larson. Copyright © 1987 by Ted W. Engstrom. Used by permission of Zondervan Publishing House.

9
Making a Commitment to Your World

"For the eyes of the Lord range throughout the earth to strengthen those whose hearts are fully committed to Him" (2 Chron. 16:9 NIV).

THE TOUCH: AN ENCOUNTER WITH SANDRA AND HELEN

I could hardly wait for the retreat to start. I was the first one to slide across the iced-over driveway to the large conference room where our two-day seminar was to be held. I wanted to get a head start setting up my materials and to get a feel of the room. I also had tucked inside the hope of fresh coffee and a warm fireplace. As soon as I entered I was greeted by coffee, a warm fire, and two women who beat me to the conference room. They too could hardly wait!

At first I thought they were the cleaning women, or maybe the cooks. They certainly did not appear to be conferees. But they were warm, outgoing, confident, and genuine in their interest in me. Yet their dress was extremely unusual. Chains and huge black belts. Tank tops and matching boots. Their hair was messy and their faces were rugged. Their arms shocked me the most. Tattoos!

"Who are these women? What are they doing here? This is a Christian women's meeting. They are nice, but they certainly don't look like any women that have been to my seminars before," I thought.

I poured a cup of coffee as I realized that these women were here by choice. As I opened my field case to pull out conference materials, they eagerly volunteered to help put materials in chairs. That is when I introduced myself.

"Good morning, I'm Marsha Spradlin."

"We know who you are," one of the women said. "We saw your picture in the brochure. We can't wait to start. That's why we are here early."

Thoughts of a room full of such women frightened me. I felt intimidated. I was not sure how to communicate, much less how well they would receive me and my contribution to the meeting. I had nothing in common with them.

Moments later the retreat coordinator walked in to greet me. I felt relief. She laughed as she invited me to a tiny office to review the schedule before the other women arrived.

"I guess you are wondering about those two."

"Wondering? Who are they?"

"They, Marsha, are among the most active and committed young Christian women in our state right now. I know that's hard to believe, but they have a testimony that has touched the lives of others like them. You know, the street people."

Jane, the conference coordinator, went on to explain.

"Sandra and Helen are sisters. I expect there will be others like them here. If I know Helen and Sandra, they have invited their friends. Anyway, Sandra and Helen grew up in a Christian home. Like so many of our kids these days, they got sidetracked in high school. Got with the wrong crowd, I guess. Before long they were skipping church, school, and family functions, like meals. That's when their parents began to get a little suspicious. Sandra and Helen had made friends with the drug culture. Well, it's a horrible story.

"Several months ago, in fact, a year ago next month, their mother was diagnosed with a terminal illness. Now, Marsha, I do not agree with this theology, but I can't knock it. I mean it worked for them.

"Sandra and Helen were, of course, upset about their mother, whom they had neglected. They decided to do what they had always been taught. They prayed. They asked God to heal their mom. In fact, they made a deal. 'God, if you make our mom well, we will get back into church.' That's the

111

part I have problems with. I mean, you can't buy favors with God. He's not a contract worker.

"Regardless, Sandra and Helen's mother did get well. A full recovery. The two girls kept their end of the 'bargain.' In fact, they rededicated their lives, gave up drugs, and began a ministry to the drug community. It is not uncommon to have two church pews filled with tattooed gals and guys in black jackets and belts at the Sunday morning worship service in their church."

As the retreat got underway, I could not help noticing the commitment of these two girls. They were determined to make a difference in their world. Was the commitment a response to fear, oughts, shoulds; or was it a response to results, desire, and love? The answer became obvious to me. Their commitment was grounded in assuming responsibility for their lost world. Such commitment resulted in action. Such actions included disciplining their life-styles. Sure, they may have looked like street people on the outside, but on the inside they were making positive steps to renew their hearts and minds. The result was in fact making a difference in the world where they lived.

Committing to Making a Difference

Sandra and Helen taught me something extraordinary. We may not be able to touch every life, but we can touch the lives of those persons nearest us in our world. To touch such lives, we cannot separate ourselves from the world physically, but we must separate ourselves spiritually. That is the winning difference. That is what made Helen and Sandra different from their non-Christian friends.

Commitment means two things. First, commitment means being dedicated to a task. Such dedication results in assuming responsibility. Commitment also means disciplining your life-style in order to accomplish your commitment and responsibility. Disciplining your life-style may mean change.

Commitment does not always make sense to us. It means separating ourselves from ourselves. Oswald Chambers said that when we commit our lives and reasoning to the attitude of Christ, such commitment takes us out of ourselves and into Christ. This moving from ourselves to Christ is not rational, but it is redemptive.

A commitment to make a difference in our world is one of the most fundamental, basic parts of the Christian life. When a person enters into a relationship with Christ, the first mark of that new relationship is a concern for uplifting other believers. Recall how Peter was admonished by Christ to feed his lambs. A Christian cares for the spiritual welfare of others.

Responsibility

How do commitment and responsibility relate? They go together like threads in a tightly woven garment. They seem to be inseparable. One strengthens the other. As we take responsibility, we demonstrate the level of our commitment. As our commitment deepens, so does our level of responsibility. Commitment can be defined as a dedication to a task. Responsibility is the action which results in such dedication.

There is a need for clarification regarding responsibility. What is our responsibility and what is God's responsibility? We cannot do what God has already done and what He alone can do. Yet God will not do what we can do. God saves us, but it is up to us to develop good habits, good character, and a proper Christian walk. We work at and respond to His salvation. We cannot save the lost, but we are responsible for communicating the message to the lost. We are responsible too for being God's available vehicle for sharing the message of salvation.

Dig deeper. Responsible means:

• Stewardship. Stewardship involves taking care of something that does not belong to us. "The task of steward is simply to properly manage something for the owner until the owner comes to take it back."[1]

• Taking action. This action is most clearly defined in the missions mandate in Matthew 28:18-20. The mandate describes the authority given to us. But with authority comes the responsibility to go, baptize, and teach all nations.

• Not taking the path of least resistance. A college roommate once said, "Marsha, by all means, don't let the crowd sway your thinking." Responsibility means doing what we know to do, in faith, even though there may be disagreement among our well-meaning supporters and friends. Seeking the path of least resistance means being the spectator in the world rather than being an active participant.

• Taking the lost condition of the world personally. I must realize that I may be the only one who can and is available to make a difference in the life of someone. The alternative is to assume that that person's life will be touched by someone other than myself.

• Recognizing comes as we realize that we may not be able to win the entire world. But we can win our world. In her book *I'm Out to Change My World*, Ann Kiemel illustrates this concept. While I can make a difference in the lives of persons I do not know through persons who represent me in other places—such as missionaries—I am not released from the responsibility to impact my world. Helen and Sandra certainly felt a responsibility to their world. Rather than running from a world of poverty and drugs, they chose to make a difference.

• Choosing every day. Joshua 24:15 (NIV) insists that we should "choose for yourselves this day whom you will serve, whether the gods your forefathers served beyond the River, or the gods of the Amorites, in whose land you are living. But as for me and my household, we will serve the Lord." Notice that the choice is not a one-time decision. It is daily. So is life. Regardless of our well-meaning intentions, it is easy to become sidetracked through daily pressures and other commitments that press into our days. For me, an early morning quiet time is the place where I make the daily decision. Often, however, I have to choose more than once each day. Life is not only daily, it is momentary. We live moment by moment.

• Accountability. First Corinthians 4:2 (NIV) is clear: "Now it is required that those who have been given a trust must prove faithful." In other words, to whom much is given, much is expected. What has God given you? You might want to take a moment to review chapter 5 on spiritual gifts and do an inventory.

The parable of the sower found in Matthew 13 is another example of accountability. Take a minute to review this parable. Pay particular attention to verses 11-12: "The knowledge of the secrets of the kingdom of Heaven has been given to you, but not to them. Whoever has will be given more, and he will have an abundance. Whoever does not have, even what he has will be taken from him." Talk about a message of accountability!

• Creativity. Does creativity seem a little out of place when discussing responsibility? I must admit, it does seem a bit unusual in such a discussion. As Christians seeking to win others to Christ, we must explore innovative methods. We must be creative. Let God be as creative with other individuals as He was with you. When I think about my own salvation experience, I think of the uniqueness of it. Sure, the plan of salvation is consistent and the same for all believers. But the outward circumstances, and even the words used to communicate a desire to know God, may be different for each individual. Creativity allows each of us to see things in a different way.

Creativity is essential in creating a positive environment for a LIVINGtouch witness. Some persons may not make the commitment to follow Jesus Christ because the gospel has been presented in such a way that there is no connection with their way of thinking. Knowledge of the Scriptures will not make a person creative. We have all known persons who knew the Scriptures and plan of salvation backward and forward, but their witness never seemed to make contact. Knowledge alone will not make a person creative. We must think about what we know in new and creative ways. Roger von Oech said in his book, *A Whack on the Side of the Head*, "Thus, the real key to being creative lies in what you do with your knowledge. Creative thinking requires an attitude or outlook which allows you to search for ideas. . . . With this outlook, you try various approaches."[2]

By adopting a creative outlook, you are open to new possibilities for changing the world for Christ. I know of no better example of the creative witness than Jesus Christ. Think about His example.

• Being yourself. You can only be the best you and second best someone else. Do you know yourself? We can only give to others in proportion to what we know about ourselves.

How well do we know ourselves? A good place to start is simply letting God search us. A word of warning. This search may not always be a happy experience. In fact, my personal "God search me" journeys have been a bit painful at times. It is never easy to have His spotlight shining directly on areas of my life badly in need of improvement. "To be found out by yourself is a terrible thing," insists Oswald Chambers.[3]

True knowledge of ourselves only can come through Him. He is the only one that can ever be unbiased or unprejudiced. Therefore, a God-examination is safe and accurate whereas a self-examination is often so cluttered with our own introspection, conceits, and even deflated sense of value that we cannot see clearly who we are and what we have to give.

Becoming yourself means becoming Him. For "I am crucified with Christ; nevertheless I live; yet not I, but Christ liveth in me" (Gal. 2:20).

• Growth. "Consider the lilies of the field, how they grow" (Luke 12:27 KJV). The word *growth* has a positive connotation. Life without growth is death. So growth is considered positive when we consider the alternatives.

I recently spent the Christmas holidays with my family in Mobile, Alabama. As each niece and nephew hugged their Aunt Bobbish, I could not help but observe the physical, emotional, and spiritual growth of each child.

Growth is not always positive. Consider the lily again. Did you know that a lily is not always in the sunshine? In fact, for the greater part of the year the lily is hidden in the earth. So how does it grow? It grows in the dark. It is in the sunlight, radiantly beautiful and sweet for only a short period of time. Perhaps that is the meaning behind the Scripture verse, "consider the lilies." We would be wise to ask ourselves: Can we be lilies unless we are willing to spend time waiting in the dark? Maybe that is where real growth occurs, the kind of growth needed to be sensitive to the hurting, hungry, and lost.

Making a commitment to the lost world also involves a—

Disciplined Life-style

A disciplined life-style reflects being a disciple.

What were the characteristics that developed and deepened each of the disciples?

First, they had an intimate relationship with the Teacher. That relationship involved walking and waiting with Him.

Second, they imitated the Teacher. This imitation involved practice, priorities, and possessing His qualities.

116

Intimate Relationship with the Teacher

• Walking with the Teacher involved getting into Jesus' stride. The real test of our intimate relationship with Jesus is not what we do in the exceptional moments of life, but what we do in the ordinary times when no one is watching or when there is nothing tremendous or exciting going on. What is a life of character? A life characteristic of His life is a life of character.

We must struggle to learn to walk with God, but when we learn to walk with Him the life of God becomes manifest in us.

Getting into His stride often is not easy. He has a different way of doing things than we do. We have to relearn to walk, and this learning is not through clinical reasoning. Walking with Him is being in an atmosphere where we get to know Him intimately. Such walking may alter our way of thinking, reasoning, and even our insights into things we never dreamed possible. That is possibility thinking.

• Waiting with the Teacher means silence. Silence makes most of us uncomfortable. There have been moments in my Christian pilgrimage when I have asked, Where are You, God? When I seem to need You most, You are silent.

God does not play hide and seek. Silence and solitude have meaning for the disciplined Christian. Often, God's silence is His answer. Why is it that we so insist on obvious answers? Greater blessing is ours when we ask with the understanding that He may choose to be silent. If God is silent with you, it may be because He is not yet ready to answer, not because He has abandoned you. Remember, God's time is not our time.

It is a wonderful thing to experience God's silence. During times of stillness we can get to know God. Likewise, we come to understand ourselves in times of silence. His silence may be the proof that He has heard!

Imitate the Teacher

• Practice. Not too many months ago two young people from a nearby church knocked on the door of one of my friends. It was Sunday afternoon. The two young people looked scared and intimidated. Finally, they dug deep within and with a weak sort of voice said:

"Hi, we're from North Main Church and we are learning how to witness. We have never done this before and we thought we would first just practice on someone. Could we practice on you before we really do it?"

My friend was a Christian, but the two young people did not know that. I thought at first, "What a clever approach." Then I realized that these two were serious. They simply wanted to practice.

A disciplined life-style means practice on and off the playing field. In fact, there really is not a place that is not a field just as there is no moment when we are not on duty. Each moment counts. Regardless of your life's vocational choice or life-style, your everyday life can become a laboratory for practice. We practice as we emulate His life every day and everywhere. Chapter 6 gives you some specific helps on how to practice making your witness count.

• Priorities. The disciplined life-style sets priorities. The first word that comes to my mind when I think of priorities is the word *time*. Chapter 7 deals with the tyranny of time as a barrier. But here let us consider time as being a meaningful priority.

There are moments when I have to make myself say, "Stop! Does God really mean for me to live like this?"

Then my inner voice asks myself, "But wasn't Christ always busy? After all, He lived a pressurized life."

I do not remember reading anywhere in the Scriptures where Jesus took time off for golf or a vacation in a nearby resort city. So where do we get a biblical basis for putting a limit on things we should or should not be doing?

Reconsider His Life-style

Though Jesus was busy, He had time for solitude when He walked or rode in a boat from one place to the next. He did take time to rest.

It is important to remember Jesus' life-style. We may well be guilty of creating our own time and priority barriers. For example, the automation of high-speed transportation, the telephone, and many other modern conveniences could be creating time to do more and more. As we do more and more, there is less time to enjoy and realize that which is important, time to have a relationship with God, and time to develop relationships with those we seek to win.

Possess the Teacher's Character

A disciplined life-style is one that emulates the life of Christ. I know of no better biblical illustration than the fruit of the spirit. To be like Him means to possess His qualities, His fruit.

"But the fruit of the Spirit is love, joy, peace, patience, kindness, goodness, faithfulness, gentleness and self-control. Those who belong to Christ Jesus have crucified the sinful nature with its passions and desires. Since we live by the Spirit, let us keep in step with the Spirit" (Gal. 5:22-25 NIV).

The fruit of the spirit is something to strive for. Unlike the gift of the spirit, which is given at the moment of salvation, the fruit may come as a package deal. To take on the total qualities of Jesus Christ means striving to obtain all of these fruits of the spirit. Only the disciplined walk with the Father leads one to produce such fruit. This fruitful, positive life-style has a magnetic effect that can make the difference in attracting others to Christ.

THE CHALLENGE TO TOUCH

Have you been challenged to touch someone's life by making a commitment to your world? Think about Helen and Sandra. Describe below how their commitment brought about change in their world. How did they demonstrate responsibility for the lost in their world?

Make the information in this chapter your own by describing ways you can impact the world simply by demonstrating a life-style of commitment. Use the questions below as a guide to explore the depths of your commitment. Write your answers in the space provided.

1. How can you demonstrate responsibility for the lost in your world?

2. In what ways can you deepen your intimate relationship with Jesus Christ which ultimately communicates your commitment?

3. What steps can you take today to imitate Him, thus standing out with a magnetic witness that counts? What about tomorrow?

---

[1] Gordon MacDonald, *Ordering Your Private World* (Nashville: Oliver-Nelson, 1985), 53.

[2] Roger von Oech, *A Whack on the Side of the Head* (New York: Warner Books, 1983), 6.

[3] Oswald Chambers, *Oswald Chambers: The Best from All His Books* (Nashville: Thomas Nelson Inc., Publishers, 1987), 314.

10
Taking Action

"But you will receive power when the Holy Spirit comes on you; and you will be my witnesses in Jerusalem, and in all Judea and Samaria, and to the ends of the earth" (Acts 1:8 NIV).

THE TOUCH: THE ENCOUNTER WITH THE LANES

She stood with a garden hose wrapped around her knees, water sprinkling on the multicolored tulips lining the front walkway. Her pose was almost statuelike, not in warm-ups or jeans, but in a silk dress and designer shoes.

"Stop!" I thought. "She's outside! This may be your only chance!"

My self-talk spoke back loud and clear as I drove past her house. "I can't. I'm already late. Surely she will be outside again one afternoon. If not, I'll just knock on her door."

I had never seen this woman before, but it was not because I had not been on the lookout. I started to think maybe the inhabitants of this old house which was surrounded by tulips and large oak trees were figments of my imagination.

I never observed any sign of human habitation. I did, however, enjoy the delightful flower garden in the front lawn.

I first noticed the house on my morning walks in my neighborhood. The neighborhood is old, established, and typically southern. It is definitely an upper class, white-collar community. The houses on my street are perched over Red Mountain with a perfect view of the valley. I am never unappreciative of the beauty. I am never unimpressed with the wealth.

I do not exactly fit in my neighborhood. I live in what I call the servant's quarters of one of these old, distinctive homes. My home is one of God's many provisions for which I am grateful. Even though I call it the servant's quarters, it is by far the most beautiful apartment I have ever had. The rent is reasonable, and the atmosphere is one of God's rich blessings to me. I thank Him often for this unique place in which to live.

As is my custom early each morning, my worn-out burgundy running shoes, with at least 5,000 miles on them, join the ranks of other fitness-conscious men and women. I do not jog. I am not into pain. Instead, I walk the same two miles each day—to the end of the street, or top of the mountain, and back.

Two doors down my street is that wonderful old house— tall columns, two stories, 16 windows, distinct architectural features. For nearly two months I had watched the restoration team strip the paint off the sides of that nearly 70-year-old house. The once strong columns were now supported by two-by-fours. Scaffolding towered over the shrubs and tulips to protect them from the debris. The house was in a period of transition.

I was not aware of the house needing repair. Yet the owners, whoever and wherever they were, must have been keenly aware of the structure's internal weaknesses. They were willing to pay the expense for having this old building repaired. The expense was more than financial. It also meant the expense of inconvenience—parking on the street rather than in their six-car garage, stepping over paint cans, and living in the house, the one with (temporarily, due to reconstruction) absolutely no aesthetic value, that was the talk of the neighborhood.

"The restoration period will be over soon," I thought one morning as I passed by. "I am sure no one will be happier than the Lanes." (I got their name from their mailbox.) "This old house will soon regain its beauty and once again become what it was intended to be."

"How symbolic," I continued to think as I walked.

"Hmm . . . This old house will regain its beauty. Such

beauty will not only be attached to the surface, but will go to the core of its foundation," I thought, as I watched the workmen remove paint inch by inch. "The result will be added strength, value, and an increased life span. Hey, what a story. This sounds like our spiritual lives. Sometimes we need spiritual restoration. Such restoration may cause changes and even inconvenience for the residents. The implications. . . ."

I rushed home, slipped off the burgundy shoes (they never come inside), grabbed a cup of coffee, and turned on my computer. I started to write an article for a missions magazine inspired from my observation.

The article was printed in the magazine four months later. By the end of the four months, the house was finished. I had an added interest in the residence because of the article. I thought often that maybe I would put a copy of my magazine in their mailbox with a thank-you note for inspiring me. The magazine could open a door. But, I was hesitant. I had never seen these people. As far as I knew, they might want to sue me for calling the house 70 years old when it was really 80 years old. I resolved to wait until the perfect opportunity.

Why do perfect opportunities have to come at such inconvenient times? I had before me the perfect opportunity. What I did not have was time. But there she was, watering the tulips. It could not have been a more rushed time for me. I was running late.

I had the responsibility for the missions program at my church that night. I still had a little preparation yet to do. The program was on "Opening Doors." The article to be used was the one I had written about the house. For that reason, I had one copy of the magazine in the backseat of my car.

"I can't stop and talk. Tomorrow I will. Right now I must go study. After all, when I do meet her, I want to give her the magazine. This will be my entry point. I only have one copy and I need it tonight!" I screamed these thoughts to myself as I drove past her house.

I got to my driveway and turned around and slowly drove back up the hill. She was still standing there with the garden hose wrapped around her knees. She looked up as I opened my car door. I am sure she wondered about me, especially when I opened the back door to the car and picked out the magazine from my briefcase.

"Another saleswoman . . . I know that's what she's thinking," I thought, as I dug deep for courage and words. "Alright, Father. You're on."

"Good afternoon Mrs. . . . ."

"Lane!" she said.

"I am your neighbor. I haven't but a minute. I am on my way to a meeting, but I have been wanting to meet you for months. I guess I haven't been able to get the courage to walk up and ring your doorbell. I know this sounds silly, but, well, I just love your house. I think it is the most beautiful house in the entire city. And remember the months of restoration? That's when I fell in love with it."

With a puzzled look she replied. "Then? That was when it was the ugliest!"

"Yes, but that's when I fell in love with it, " I insisted.

Mrs. Lane continued to stand there with this most enchanting expression on her face as water soaked the tulips.

"You see, before most people are even awake, I am on my morning walk. Each morning I would pass your house. I saw the slow but consistent progress. I watched the workmen remove the paint inch-by-inch from those old columns. Well, it inspired me. So I wrote an article about it for a magazine. I have been wanting to give you a copy, but I never saw anyone home until today. Anyway, here it is. Would you like to have a copy?"

Suddenly the blank, enchanting stare turned into a brilliant smile.

"Well, yes! What did you say your name is?"

"Oh, I forgot, I'm Marsha Spradlin. I live two doors down—the second house on the left."

"Marsha, I just love knowing my neighbors. Surely you have a minute to come inside. After all, if you are that inspired with the outside of the house, you must come inside." (I felt another article coming . . . "Come Inside.")

"I really must go. My meeting is within minutes." Deep within I was almost preoccupied with my meeting. I thought, "What meeting? You have just given your magazine away. You'll have to wing it tonight, Spradlin."

"I promise. I will not keep you but a moment," Mrs. Lane insisted.

She swung open the door. I followed.

"Dave, we have a guest."

Dave, Mr. Lane, came rushing down the spiral staircase. He welcomed me as if I were his own daughter. Mrs. Lane explained who I was and about the article.

"Oh, Marsha, let us give you a tour," Mr. Lane insisted.

"I really can't. Not today. But I would love to come again."

"Nonsense, I'll give you the tour now," he said, as he escorted me through the 20-room house. I looked and awed and churned inside. Suddenly I realized: Now is the only time there is. The door of opportunity was wide open. I had been seeking entrance, yet my priority that moment was to prepare so that I would do well at my meeting. These people are what "the meeting" is all about. I relaxed, walked slowly, and gave the Lanes my undivided attention.

After the tour we chatted a few minutes before I left. I learned about their children, the history of the house, their hobbies, and the interests of these charming people.

"Now, exactly what do you do?" Dave asked.

I shared briefly about my work. Since the couple had no previous church experience, I could tell it was difficult for them to understand my work. "My favorite part is writing articles about special people like you! Better go," I said.

"Oh yes, you have that meeting. You will come again, won't you?" Mrs. Lane asked.

"May I?"

"Our door is always open."

We exchanged good-byes and I left.

Needless to say, I was late for church and totally unprepared. Yet, in a real sense, some preparation, the meaningful kind, had been done. Instead of our usual program, I told the group about my experience with the Lanes. The group of young women prayed for open doors of opportunities and for the ability to take action even at the most inconvenient moments.

It has been six months. I have not seen the Lanes since that spring day. It's cold outside—midwinter. But each morning as I walk up the street in a bundle of coats and gloves, I pass the old house. A day never passes that I do not remember hearing Mrs. Lane saying, "Our door is always open."

I then find myself asking, "When are you going back? Will you ever take action?" Now is the only time there is. What should be my motivation to take action? What's stopping me?[1]

Do It Now!

Webster defines the word *action* as "the doing of something; state of being in motion or of working; an act or things done."[2] This time I agree wholeheartedly with Webster's definition of "the doing of something." But notice that he places no time frame on when the doing is to be done. You have learned that now is the only time there is. So, the "doing" must be done now!

What is stopping us? Somewhere in the back of my mind I remember a college physics professor making a statement about motion and action. "For every action there is an equal and opposite reaction." Of course, my physics professor was talking about the law of motion. When there is a moving object, there must be an equal force in order to stop the object. Without the equal force, there is a collision. We have all experienced some form of collision in our lifetimes.

I think we as Christians have taken the law of physics and somehow twisted, tied, or applied it to our Christian lives. If I act, there will be an equal and opposite reaction. I call that fear. Fear could be one answer to the question, What's stopping us? We must fear an equal and opposite reaction. While this law of motion may apply to the physical world, it in no way applies to our spiritual worlds. Instead, the opposite is true. For every action we take in being a witness, there is the potential for an equal and positive reaction or response!

Face it. Many of us are still immobilized by fear.

We discussed obstacles in chapter 7. Fear of failure was certainly one of the obstacles. But we may need to dig deeper into other immobilizing factors before we can determine what will get us started witnessing and keep us going.

Many of us are plagued with negative thinking and antici-pation of that equal and opposite reaction. In most cases, however, that which we fearfully anticipate does not exist. When we worry about rejection, we are living through an event before it has actually happened.

Have you ever noticed the expression, "It's too good to be true"? Why could we not turn that experience around to be "It's too good, it must be true!" To realize fully our potential we must add action to our hope. "Faith without actions is nothing." Too many of us live on "Someday I'll . . ."; "Someday I'll be that witness . . .," we say. But someday never comes. It never has and it never will come.

To me to experience God's potential as a LIVINGtouch witness, we must first master the ability to take action. Taking action does not mean we produce results. He produces the results. But until we take action, we will not experience His power.

On a trip to the East I roomed with a friend who experienced great frustration one morning putting on her makeup. With two of us sharing the bathroom, Marti decided to let me have the big mirror as she took her little compact mirror and "put on her face" by a tiny lamp near the bed. Frustrated by the lack of light, she made this remark, "A three-way lamp and a one-way bulb." I said nothing, but thought, "Hmm, that reminds me of our potential as Christians. That three-way lamp was designed to give three levels of brightness. Because the light bulb placed in the lamp was only capable of one level of brightness, Marti was only able to get a limited amount of light from it. The lamp was unable to realize the full extent of its potential."

God has gifted us with tremendous potential. We have the potential to be that three-way lamp. Yet how often do we use only a part of the potential He has given us.

We may be stopped because we have not recognized fully our potential. Or we are not using the potential we have recognized. For various reasons we limit that potential. We say, "I just can't do that as well as she can"; "I'm just too shy"; "I am not as educated, talented, or as attractive"; or, "That's just not me." Other excuses include, "I don't have time"; "No one appreciates what I do anyway." Each excuse represents a reason, not a result. Each negative thought represents that one-way bulb that will prevent us from shining our brightest.[3]

God has such wonderful opportunities for us if we are willing to see them. It is not until we take action, however, that we experience His power within. God's most celebrated blessings come through our being our natural selves, simply living out our potential. Perhaps we need to put three-way bulbs in our lamps to light up our lives and illuminate the lives of those around us with His love.

"No one lights a lamp and hides it in a jar or puts it under a bed. Instead, he puts it on a stand, so that those who come in can see the light" (Luke 8:8:16 NIV).

We all want results. Without results there is only despair. You can deny it, pretend that it is not true, but that does not change the fact that as Christians we are made to want results in winning our world to Christ. We are simply born that way.

We want to reach our potential as Christians. But do you know any Christian who has? Consider the verses from Philippians: "Brothers, I do not consider myself yet to have taken hold of it" (Phil. 3:13 NIV).

Warning: Do not become so conscious that you will never "take hold of it" that you become immobilized and give up the actions toward the goal. Such feelings result in self-hate. These feelings are focused on self rather than on others. We must learn to relax, enjoy the thrill of the journey of "taking hold of it," and realize our potential as LIVINGtouch witnesses.

We will not experience action and results by reading books, going to seminars, and listening to tapes. Certainly, these experiences can lead to action, but they are not the results of action. The more action we take, the more results we experience. The more results we experience, the more we realize who we are and Whose we are in Christ.

Taking action does not mean work. It is harder to *not* be than to be when you are rightly related to Christ. Being an active participant in God's plan is our natural state. The idea that it is difficult or complicated to be a witness is an idea from the world's belief system.

God has already equipped us with all that we need for being a witness. It is a paradox. We must accept it before we have it.

We cannot get started until we know what we want. If you are not sure where in your world to start, do not stop, just start somewhere doing something. If it is wrong, you will find out. You can make corrections and call the experience "failing forward."

Could it be that we are so into the habit of listening to what others want us to do, that we no longer hear what the Father wants? Take time to listen to the Father. In your quiet time each day ask yourself this question, What would I like to see happen in my world today? Then jot down what you can do to make this happen. The emphasis is on starting. Too many of us wait for our ships to come in when we never launched them in the first place. When the ship does come in, or an opportunity to witness does fall into our lives, we are too scared to unload the ship, or act upon the opportunity.

Sometimes we must unlearn. We all have tendencies to handle situations over and over again in the same way. We do not let our creative abilities work through us as witnesses. We must give up our belief systems about the way witnessing should or has always worked before and look for new ways, opportunities, channels, and options to witness creatively. Witnessing calls for dependence on the Holy Spirit. Witnessing may well be the movement of the Holy Spirit within us.

When we give up the idea of how the results should be, we can participate in a witnessing experience without fear. We only become frustrated in personal witnessing when our ideal of *how* witnessing has to be does not match up with the way witnessing is. When we give up our idea of how witnessing has to be, and rely on the Holy Spirit to be the director of our lives, we are freed to realize a new dimension of what we can do, where we can go, who can come into our lives, as well as what we can be as witnesses.

Personal witnessing is not a matter of being a success or a failure. Successful personal witnessing encounters are those in which we look at every rejection as a friend and as an opportunity to learn, change, and gain new insights for the next opportunity.

Getting started is the first step. It starts the pendulum swinging. This first step comes from motivation.

What is motivation and how can we obtain it? Actually, the two—motivation and getting started—are woven together. The more action we take, the stronger is our motivation.

Motivation is the inner drive and impulse to act because of

a cause. It's an incentive to reach a goal. It is personal quality that prods us from a position of inertia toward movement, change, and action.

While there is infinite material written about motivation, motivation cannot be bought, taught, or even given away. Experts in motivational science differ on whether we can actually motivate another person. They believe that motivation must come from within a person. We are motivated by two sources: external (extrinsic) and internal (intrinsic). The internal form is thought to be the higher, more lasting, form of motivation. Both kinds of motivation, however, lead to action. You cannot have results without action. People with goals know that action is required to meet those goals.

Driving the speed limit is a good example of external motivation. I know I ought to drive within the limits. I do so to keep from getting a ticket. But if there were no such thing as tickets, speed traps, or speed limits, I would probably drive faster. I am motivated to drive a certain way to avoid getting caught. My motivation causes me to act in a certain way that can have positive results. This form of motivation comes from the oughts and shoulds, rather than the want to's.

Some people witness from this external motivation. Their motivation comes from outside of themselves. They feel they *should*. Maybe they are motivated to witness because of guilt. Maybe they have observed the "white fields." While this action may be positive and have positive results, internal (or intrinsic) motivation is a higher and more effective form of motivation. Internal motivation often has more eternal implications!

The person who witnesses out of the conviction that he or she is called to be a witness is the person operating from the internal form of motivation.

Internal motivation starts with a proper relationship with the Father. It is He who gives us the desire and the readiness to take action. When we are ready to serve the Father, no task is too small or too big. We are ready, no matter what. Being ready means being ready for sudden surprise visits from God.

The internally motivated take initiative to witness. They do not hesitate when God speaks nor do they question what He has said. Take the initiative, stop vacillating, and make the first move. Be firm when God speaks, act in faith immediately on His command, and never change your mind. Take action, step forward with your will now, never go back. Burn your bridges behind you. We have to begin where we are, not where we would like to be.

The emphasis on motivation is simply action. The motivated person "pairs nouns with verbs: he determines his goals (nouns) and acts to achieve them (verbs)."[4]

Spiritually motivated persons who are dedicated to making a witness in their world

1. think positively about themselves and all witnessing opportunities;
2. expect the best and always try to do their best; witnessing means being prepared;
3. keep their goals in focus, but are flexible enough to adjust their goals when needed;
4. look forward each day to opportunities; look in each day for opportunities to be a LIVINGtouch;
5. maintain healthy self-concepts and belief that *we* can make a difference in our world.

What keeps us going? The only way to get started and to keep going in a world that seems to bombard us constantly for time and priorities is through a solid commitment to witness.

What is commitment? It is easier to describe commitment than to define it. *Promise, submit, permit, mission, remit* are cousins to the word *commit*. *Send* or *let go* in Latin is *mitto* and *missue*. Combined with *come, commit* means "to send together." The prefix and root do not work alone; neither do you.[5]

Commitment is . . .
    not trying but accomplishing.
    changing maybe into certainly.
    putting others first without a second thought.
    sharing good news even when it's old to you.
    doing things that please an absent friend.
    leaving a warm bed when a small voice says, "I'm cold."

enjoying a visit before you've gone and after you return.

learning to love the things you hate to do.

burning your bridges behind you, not in front of you.

aiming at a target that most people cannot even see and hitting it.

life sharing.[6]

A commitment could involve changing the way you look at yourself—your potential, gifts, abilities, skills—and your world. Commitment could be the key which unlocks our immobility toward mere existence. Commitment is the quality which gives enthusiasm for life. A committed person is the opposite of the bored, cynical-type person. Commitment challenges us to a new way of living. It frees us from the shackles of those self-destructive and debilitating attitudes of "I can't" or "I won't."

If you have lost your compassion for a world that is sick, hungry, and dying, you can discover that commitment to God's great plan for the salvation and healing of all people will separate you from the *driven*, those externally motivated, toward the *called*, those internally and eternally motivated.

Commitment means getting up after falling down, starting over, being persistent because you know your cause is right. Commitment means not being afraid of pain. Some of the most painful experiences I have had have been encounters with people like those shared in this book.

Theodore Roosevelt engraved on the minds of many the meaning of commitment when he said it is better to have some triumphs, though checkered by failure, than to belong to the host of beings who experience neither joy nor sorrow and live a colorless existence where such things have no place. Like motivation, commitment cannot be separated from action.

To what are we committed? Is there anything that means everything to us? What are we living for? Have you deliberately committed your will to Jesus Christ?

The word *commitment* means "to work together." We must be a part of an unbroken chain of continuous commitments. We are designed for commitment. We are keys to the personal fulfillment of God and the eternal salvation of our world.

132

Winning the world, therefore, will take all of us. Anything short of all of us will diminish the sacrifice and commitment made by Jesus Christ 2,000 years ago. Jesus knew what He was doing, even though no one else did. He knew that His commitment would lead Him ultimately to a hill outside Jerusalem where He would be scandalized in public. This man was no pale Galilean. Instead, Jesus was committed to a miracle. As kingdom citizens, we must be so committed to Him that we keep on keeping on even though no one else understands our motivation or the reason for our commitment. His love for humanity was so great that He knowingly gave up His life to give us eternal relationship with Him. Do we dare exhibit this Jesus-style commitment? You do not have to be a great person to be committed. "Yes," you say. "But Jesus was a great person." Remember that great people are ordinary people with an extraordinary amount of commitment.

The Father has invested much in you and me so that we might have the ability to keep the chain unbroken. Our commitment to be a LIVINGtouch can be the key that not only opens the gate to vast new fields of opportunity to witness, but opens Heaven's gates for countless others as well. Commitment linked with action means results. Some results are obvious, others are not.

As I am committed to His task, I experience personal growth and realize the capacity to grow even more. I experience internal peace. My action is the direct result of my decision to be committed. There is no peace in indecision.

Commitment, then, means discovering purpose as you discover your reason for living. It means a daily recommitment of self to the cause. It means experiencing the taste or thrill of victory from having led a precious soul to the Father's kingdom. We must be ready to lead these souls to do the same, to witness to others. How do you become committed?

1. Make a decision *now* to make a difference. You can!
2. Act upon your decision. Do not be intimidated by the fear of change.
3. Continue to act. Remember that life is daily. So is commitment.

Commitment is where living really begins. Start living by committing yourself to being a winning witness.

In *A Time for Commitment,* Ted W. Engstrom outlines seven practical steps to help change the world. Each step is saturated in commitment:

1. Make your personal commitment to change your world.
2. Ask God to give you greater sensitivity to the needs of those around you.
3. Search the Scriptures to learn how God Himself sees humanity.
4. Remember that the world includes your neighbor or spouse, as well as people in other countries.
5. Ask God to guide you in knowing how to work to change the world.
6. Take one step at a time. Act now upon what you know, even while you ask God to show you more.
7. Be patient and steadfast.[7]

What are we committed to? What are we waiting for? The mandate is clear:

"Go therefore and make disciples of all nations, baptizing them in the name of the Father and of the Son and of the Holy Spirit, teaching them to observe all that I have commanded you; and lo, I am with you always, to the close of the age" (Matt. 28:19-20 RSV).

Join me in being committed to being a LIVINGtouch witness to change the world for Christ.

THE CHALLENGE TO TOUCH

Do a personal What's Stopping You? inventory. Write down everything you can think of that is keeping you from being an effective witness. Write your list in column 1. In column 3 write your goals. Review chapter 7 if needed. In the middle column write down steps taken to *stop* that which is *stopping* you from reaching your goals.

Now do a motivational inventory. Ask yourself these questions:
1. What/Who motivates me?
2. When am I most excited?
3. How can taking action increase my motivation to be a winning witness?

Finally, do a commitment inventory. In the space provided list everything that comes to mind regarding your current personal commitments. The following questions can help you get started: Where does personal witnessing fit in my life? What actions do I need to take in order to make personal witnessing a priority?

[1]Marsha Spradlin, "Laser," *Contempo*, June 1987, 41.
[2]*Webster's New World Dictionary of the American Language*, 2d college ed., s.v. "action."
[3]Marti Solomon, "Highlights," *Accent*, January 1988.
[4]George Shinn, *The Miracle of Motivation* (Wheaton, IL: Tyndale House Publishers, Inc., 1981), 13.
[5]Taken from *A Time for Commitment* by Ted W. Engstrom with Robert C. Larson. Copyright © 1987 by Ted W. Engstrom. Used by permission of Zondervan Publishing House.
[6]Ibid.
[7]Ibid.

Evangelism Resources

Office of Spiritual Awakening
The Shantung Revival—Book written by C. L. Culpepper, the story of revival in the Shantung Province of North China, one of the greatest revivals in modern history. (202-05P; $1.49)
God's Divine Work—Book by Lewis A. Drummond on the history and principles of biblical revival and spiritual awakening. (202-07P; $1.49)
Spiritual Awakening—Book by Bob Eklund, giving a historical and biblical overview of spiritual awakenings. (202-21P; $1.49)
Intercessory Prayer—Book by James C. K. McClure, providing a scriptural foundation for intercession. (202-13P; $1.49)

Evangelism Church Growth Department
Tracts to use in leading people to Christ
The Real Life (212-08P; $.10)
Eternal Life booklet (212-64P; $.10)
A Word of Help for the Unsaved (223-86F; free)
Christ the Only Hope (223-87F; free)
Some Things God Wants You to Know (223-89F; free)
What Am I Responsible For? (223-90F; free)
Who Am I? (223-91F; free)
What Is God Like? (223-94F; free)

Mass Evangelism Department
Preparation Through Prayer—A monthlong guide for Bible reading, leading to personal growth. (211-07P; $6.00 per 100)
Personal Commitment Guide—A guide to use when counseling people making life-changing decisions. (211-28P; $6.00 per 100)
Sweet Hour of Prayer Spiritual Preparation Guide—A guide for individual spiritual inventory, leading to personal renewal. (211-51P; $.50)

Series of pamphlets to give to people making life-changing decisions
Life Commitment (Special Service) (211-09P; $6.00 per 100)
A New Dimension (Rededication) (211-10P; $6.00 per 100)
Toward Christian Maturity (How to Grow Spiritually) (211-11P; $6.00 per 100)
Your New Life (For the New Believer) (211-12P; $6.00 per 100)

Prices are subject to change.

Make check or money order payable to the Home Mission Board and send to
Customer Service Center
Home Mission Board
1350 Spring Street, NW
Atlanta, GA 30367-5601

Or call: **1 (800) 634-2462**

Bibliography

Aldrich, Joseph C. *Life-style Evangelism*. Portland: Multnomah Press, 1981.

Arn, Win, and Arn, Charles. *The Master's Plan for Making Disciples*. Pasadena: Church Growth Press, 1982.

Bennett, Dink. *Living Reflections*. Cincinnati: Standard Publishing Co., 1975.

Blackwell, Muriel Fontenot. *The Keeping Shelf*. Nashville: Broadman Press, 1985.

Bright, Bill. *Witnessing Without Fear*. San Bernardino: Here's Life Publishers, Inc., 1987.

Chambers, Oswald. *Oswald Chambers: The Best from All His Books*. Nashville: Thomas Nelson Inc., Publishers, 1987.

_____. *My Utmost for His Highest*. New York: Dodd, Mead and Company, 1935.

Clemmons, William P. *Discovering the Depths*. Nashville: Broadman Press, 1987.

Collins, Gary R. *The Magnificent Mind*. Grand Rapids: Baker Book House, 1985.

Dickson, Elaine. *Say No, Say Yes to Change*. Nashville: Broadman Press, 1982.

Eims, LeRoy. *Winning Ways*. Wheaton, IL: Victor Books, 1979.

Elliot, Elisabeth. *Discipline: The Glad Surrender*. Old Tappan, NJ: Fleming H. Revell, Co., 1982.

Engstrom, Ted W. *Motivation to Last a Lifetime*. Grand Rapids: Zondervan Publishing House, 1984.

Engstrom, Ted W., with Robert C. Larson. *A Time for Commitment*. Grand Rapids: Zondervan Publishing House, 1987.

Gordon, Arthur. *Touch of Wonder*. Old Tappan, NJ: Fleming H. Revell, Co., 1979.

Greer, E. Eugene, and Greer, Elaine W. *Daily Guide Toward Fitness*. Nashville: Broadman Press, 1981.

Guralnik, David B., ed. *Webster's New World Dictionary of the American Language*. New York: Simon and Schuster, 1982.

Joiner, Barbara. *Yours for the Giving: Spiritual Gifts*. Birmingham: Woman's Missionary Union, 1986.

MacDonald, Gordon. *Ordering Your Private World*. Nashville: Oliver-Nelson, 1985.

——————. *Restoring Your Spiritual Passion*. Nashville: Oliver-Nelson, 1986.

Mandino, Og. *The Greatest Miracle in the World*. New York: Bantam Books, 1979.

Maples, Donna. *Friends Are for Helping*. Birmingham: New Hope, 1986.

Pippert, Rebecca, and Siemens, Ruth. *Evangelism*. Downers Grove, IL: Inter-Varsity Press, 1985.

Pippert, Rebecca Manley. *Out of the Salt Shaker*. Downers Grove, IL: Inter-Varsity Press, 1979.

Raines, Robert. *To Kiss the Joy*. Nashville: Abingdon Press, 1983.

Reed, Wilma. "Everything You Need." *Contempo* (October 1986): 11.

Schulz, Charles. Peanuts featuring "Good Ol' Charlie Brown." United Features Syndicate, Inc., 1981.

Shinn, George. *The Miracle of Motivation*. Wheaton, IL: Tyndale House Publishers, Inc., 1981.

Solomon, Marti. "Highlights." *Accent* (January 1988).

Spradlin, Marsha. "My Bold-Witnessing Experience." *Start* (October-November-December 1986): cover 3.

——————. "Laser." *Contempo* (February 1987): 41.

——————. "Laser." *Contempo* (June 1987): 41.

——————. "Laser." *Contempo* (May 1988): 56.

——————. *Transformed One Winter*. Nashville: Broadman Press, 1989.

Swindoll, Charles R. *Living Above the Level of Mediocrity.* Waco: Word Inc., 1987.

The One Year New Testament. Wheaton, IL: Tyndale House Publishers, Inc., 1987.

The 2:7 Series. Colorado Springs: Navpress, 1979.

Thompson, W. Oscar, Jr., and Thompson, Carolyn. *Concentric Circles of Concern.* Nashville: Broadman Press, 1981.

Torrey, R. A. *How to Bring Men to Christ.* Minneapolis: Bethany House, 1977.

Von Oech, Roger. *A Whack on the Side of the Head.* New York: Warner Books, 1983.

Waitley, Denis. *The Winner's Edge.* New York: Berkley Publishing, 1983.